Maley Bainbridge Crist

Patchwork

The Poems and Prose Sketches of Maley Bainbridge Crist

Maley Bainbridge Crist

Patchwork

The Poems and Prose Sketches of Maley Bainbridge Crist

ISBN/EAN: 9783744685115

Printed in Europe, USA, Canada, Australia, Japan

Cover: Foto ©Thomas Meinert / pixelio.de

More available books at **www.hansebooks.com**

PATCHWORK

THE POEMS AND PROSE
SKETCHES OF........
MALEY BAINBRIDGE CRIST

ATLANTA
THE MARTIN & HOYT COMPANY
THE DIXIE PRESS
1898

Copyright, 1898, by
MALEY BAINBRIDGE CRIST

⁎ *The publication of this complete edition of Mrs. Crist's works is made possible by the courtesy of the Frank Leslie's Monthly, who originally published several of Mrs. Crist's poems and sketches.*

Illustrations designed by
MRS. DAVID BOTT MANLEY

TO MY PRECIOUS SON,
LUCIEN BAINBRIDGE CRIST,
WHOSE YOUNG LIFE IS THE POESY OF MY EXISTENCE;
AND TO MY DEAR MOTHER,
LUCRETIA WRIGHT BAINBRIDGE,
WHO DAILY GAVE MY CHILDISH SOUL INSPIRATION
FOR LIFE'S HIGHEST IDEALS,
I DEDICATE THESE TALES AND RHYMES,
SKETCHED IN THE LEISURE MOMENTS OF A BUSY LIFE.
— Maley Bainbridge Crist.

"Keep thy heart with all diligence, for out of it are the issues of life."

AUTHOR'S PREFACE

* * *

"Do not trouble yourself too much about the light on your statue," said Michael Angelo to the young sculptor, "the light of the public square will test its value."

CONTENTS "PATCHWORK"

STORIES

	PAGE
THE WOMAN'S STORY OF TOLSTOI'S KREUTZER SONATA,	15
ROMANCE OF A KENTUCKIAN IN ST. AUGUSTINE,	57
LITTLE JEAN'S THEFT,	77
NUMBER FOURTEEN,	81
CATHERINE,	91
THE EXPERIENCE OF A CORPSE, OR THE FIRST NIGHT UNDER GROUND,	115
LOVE'S FIRST CONQUEST. (Leggendario),	131
A CONFEDERATE FOR A DAY,	139
THE TWO HAT PINS,	149
A CHAPTER FROM A BOY'S LIFE,	157
HOW THE CAPTAIN FOUND HIS SERVANT,	165
THE BRIDAL CHAMBER OF FLORIDA'S SILVER SPRINGS,	173

POEMS

TEMPTATION,	187
VILLANELLE. (The Jasmines' Message),	191
I MISS YOU SO,	192
MISSISSIPPI ON THE GULF,	193

Contents "Patchwork"

	PAGE
WHY DANDELIONS TURN GRAY,	194
LINES TO A BEAUTIFUL GIRL,	197
AWAY DOWN IN GEORGIA,	198
PROTEST,	200
VILLANELLE,	201
THE STARS AND BARS,	202
ONENESS,	204
ECHO,	206
WHAT HER SISTER THOUGHT,	208
CLEOPATRA,	209
RETROSPECTION,	211
REGRET,	213
INFINITE,	217
A DARK NIGHT,	219
GOLD *vs.* LOVE,	221
LINES TO MY MOTHER,	223
CONTENT,	225
CHASTENED,	227
REVERY,	228
"I AM THE WAY,"	230
FLORIDA, QUEEN OF THE SOUTH,	232
LINES RESPECTFULLY DEDICATED TO GENERAL J. J. DICKISON,	233
THE RED, RED ROSE,	235
HOW DO I LOVE YOU?	236
TRUST,	237

LIST OF ILLUSTRATIONS

	PAGE
Maley Bainbridge Crist . . . . . *Frontispiece*	
He Lifted Me from the Coffin as though I Had Been a Child	47
I Love You; and You — You Love Her. . . .	64
The Slight, Beautifully Rounded Figure of a Young Girl.	66
Yours is a Curious Theft, this Stealing Flowers .	78
Fair Summer Knew Her Power, Coquettishly She Turned Away	137
One was a Jeweled Thing of Beauty, the Other a Confederate Button, Bearing the S. C. Coat of Arms	149
Flowers are God's Pretty Little Thoughts, Mamma	157
I Feel as if I Could Follow that Melody, if I had a Flute	162
With Compliments of the Author to the Many Friends Desiring this Photo	185
Temptation —"Behold! the image cold seemed to have grown Into real life — a woman, sweet and fair."	187
Temptation —"The fair dream picture vanished from his view, And with it, sin cast off her blooming mask."	188
Temptation —"They gazed upon the priest in fear and awe, Amazed at the angelic look he wore." . .	190
Stars and Bars— "It shall live in song and story, Though its folds are in the dust."	202

It is gratifying to know that the public is to be favored with a collection of Mrs. Crist's writings.

It is only a fair encouragement to the talent and labor of the writer for me to express the hope that "Patchwork" will be cordially received by the public. Stamped as it is with her personality and of southern inspiration, I believe it will be so received by that people who are ever ready to recognize grace and reward effort.

WASHINGTON, D. C., January 28, 1898.

PATCHWORK

THE WOMAN'S STORY OF TOLSTOI'S KREUTZER SONATA

CHAPTER I.

WITHOUT doubt, no class of men are so well versed in psychological analysis as the priesthood, for to them is laid bare the human conscience with its mysterious promptings and consciousness of guilt in motive or act. The sins of their people become a powerful educator, not alone deepening their insight and broadening their sympathy for frail humanity, but lifting them, as well, to a higher and more exalted plane of life. Father Wayneclete, the venerable and venerated Benedictine whose life of labor and love elicited the devotion of all with whom he came in contact, was a superior example of this class of men. His sincere earnestness, his singular asceticism, combined with great wisdom and courage, and, above all else, the most divine spirit of charity which marked his dealings with his fellow-men, stamped him an extraordinary personage. For ten years Father Wayneclete had been in charge of a monastery in a certain small village in England. Situated less than a mile from the monastery, stood a convent where for thirty years had dwelt a nun in whose seemingly quiet and uneventful life there might never have been revealed a past, save for the presence of this monk. At a table in a chamber of the convent sat the nun. Some way—the bare room, with its lack of the touches of femininity, was in keeping with her presence. The rigid folds of her coarse serge gown seemed to accentuate, rather than detract from the beauty of a figure which might have served as a Grecian model. She seemed torn by intensity of feeling. Her bosom heaved convulsively, and gazing upward she exclaimed aloud: "Holy Mother, pity me! I must express my feelings, or I shall go mad." Catching up pen and paper, her trembling hand glided rapidly across the sheets; and like one demented, she murmured aloud the sentences which tossed themselves from her burning brain. Her voice was hoarse with emotion, as she followed aloud these tracings of her pen. "In the seclusion of my convent chamber, my rebellious hand dares pen thoughts and deeds which should long since have been wiped from memory. In this, I may be committing an unpardonable sin — but it is a partial escape from self, and a possible rescue from insanity. For thirty years, none have ever guessed the wild war which has waged in my heart, and which neither time, solitude, nor religion, have the power to subdue. My religious duties are a hollow mockery, and my life a living lie; for during all the outward calm of these years of convent life, there has rankled in my heart, where naught but love and peace should reign, a hatred both fierce and bitter; hatred toward *man*, the author of all my woe — *man*, in whom for thirty years I have believed goodness and sincerity to be but a myth, an ideal element bestowed by deluded women. It is hard for one who has suffered as I have to brand them-

selves a hypocrite, and yet such I feel myself to be, for I have entered the Confessional during all these years, without once unburdening my soul of its past sins. Even now, when upon the very brink of despair, my proud heart rebels against revealing itself to man, and I hesitate, even though mine own eyes have witnessed the unselfish and self-sacrificing life of this Benedictine, Father Wayneclete. Woman! surely thy name is *inconsistency*. Wherefore, after thirty years of hatred and distrust toward man, should the white flower of faith blossom, and I eagerly stretch forth my hands to welcome the first opportunity of baring my poor scarred heart before this monk, for he compels both confidence and respect."
She stopped suddenly, and rising to her feet, rent the manuscript into a thousand fragments, exclaiming as she did so: "It is all *useless, useless;* I can but find relief in the unburdening of my soul of its sins. I must save myself from insanity, and this is my last, my only resort." She hesitated for a moment only, and then, trembling violently, stole softly from the convent, and down the dark avenue of trees,

leading to the monastery of the Benedictine. So intent was she upon her purpose, that of finding the sympathy which now alone could sustain poor tottering reason, that a sense of impropriety in thus stealing away to the monastery never entered her mind, nor did the fact that she might encounter other monks than Father Wayneclete. Onward sped the slight dark-robed figure which might easily have been confounded with the shadows of the night. Onward, and still onward, never pausing until she reached and ascended the steps of the monastery Cathedral. The human mind is so constituted as often to observe, and, as it were, amuse itself with the most minute and trivial surroundings at times when its greatest interests are at stake. And so this nun, who shrank into the darkest corner of the dimly-lighted cathedral, mechanically noted the gold embroidered cloth, and quaintly carved candlesticks of the altar; noted the heavy crimson curtain of the Confessional, the pictures along the nave, and even the faint perfume of the lilies which decked the altar of the Virgin before which knelt the aged Benedictine, upon whose help she now so absolutely depended; then, slowly her mind wandered back to the object of her visit, and she wondered, shudderingly, if this man would be able to save her from herself. The church was deserted, save for the presence of these two. She was incapable of judging the length of time that elapsed before the monk ceased his devotion, and moved slowly down the aisle of the church. She was too greatly excited to speak, and seized the sleeve of his surtout much as a child might have done. He started perceptibly. The presence of a nun in this monastic precinct was a thing unheard of; and yet his manner was kindly, and his voice sympathetic as he inquired: "What can I do for you, my daughter!" The poor creature seemed suffering bodily, as well as mentally, and for an instant the small bloodless hands with their scarred fingers, were pressed closely against the left side, while a spasm of pain contracted the features, which notwithstanding the ravages of age and suffering, together with the deep and lasting scars which appealed pitifully to an observer, still bore unmistakable traces of beauty. The monk noted all this and also that the face was that of a Russian, as he caught in his arms the fainting figure, which must otherwise have fallen at his feet.

CHAPTER II.

FATHER WAYNECLETE was now thoroughly alarmed, for the face of his strange guest in the dimly-lighted cathedral seemed to bear the gray ashy whiteness of a corpse. Not caring to arouse the inmates of the monastery, and thereby perhaps divulge a secret intended for himself alone, he labored patiently with his charge, chafing the small, cold hands, and forcing stimulants between the colorless lips, until he was rewarded by her return to consciousness. She sat up, and gazing about in a bewildered way, would have spoken, but for the interposition of the monk. "Wait, daughter. Do not try to speak until you are stronger!" he exclaimed; and she obeyed with the docility of a child. For some moments they sat thus, when the nun broke the silence by exclaiming in a voice so pensive, so soft and sweet, that it was like the notes of a bird, or the soft ripple of water. "Father, I have come to you, that you may save me from myself." "Daughter," replied the monk, "I will gladly offer you my sympathy and assistance by pointing you to the sacrament of penance, that you may make your peace with God." "Father," she continued, "for thirty years I have entered the Confessional without once revealing the burdens of my scarred heart. My life has been a living lie. But the hour has come when I must unburden my soul of its sins, and find forgiveness. Nay, more — I must have something tangible. I must have warm human sympathy; for let my sins be what they may, my suffering has been such that I cannot bear reproach; and you — you are the only one to whom I feel I can confide the story of my life." "Though your sins be as scarlet, they shall be white as snow." Softly the beautiful promise of God fell from the lips of the monk, and soothed the aching heart of the grief-stricken nun beside him. A heavy sigh shook her form as she replied: "Never was there an experience like mine; never a life more desolate; and never, perchance, a life hurled into eternity by the stroke of a dagger, and brought back by a kiss, a caress, a kindly word. Ah! how empty all that seems to me now! But I digress. To begin my story, I was the daughter of a landed gentleman of Penza whose fortune was ruined by unwise speculation. I was most tenderly and delicately reared. Educated in a convent, breathing from infancy, as it were, the spirituality of my surroundings, I was graduated at an early age without having entered into the slightest contact with the practical and materialistic outside world. My nature being both poetical and hypersensitive, became abnormally so, nurtured by such surroundings; and my introduction to society, found me as guileless and unsuspicious as a little child, and equally as ready to clothe whomsoever fancy might dictate with attributes existing alone in my own imagination. Just as my education was completed, the reverses in my father's fortune occurred; but although dowerless, I found myself surrounded by admirers, for I was what the world called beautiful and my accomplishments were more than ordinary. My life was smooth and uneventful until there crossed its pathway the man destined forever to curse it—one Posdnicheff. But how the name startles you! You have heard the story, then, of Posdnicheff the wife murderer? Aye! but you have heard only one side of it; the other I am about to relate to you. But compose yourself, father. You are white like death; you tremble and your teeth chatter. You are not in the presence of a spirit, but in that of the wife of whom not alone Posdnicheff, but all who have heard his story, believe to be in her grave." "Proceed, daughter," replied the monk, with a desperate effort at composure. "This Posdnicheff," she continued, "created upon me a different impression than had any of my other admirers. There was a suave deference in his manner toward women, mingled with certain easy nonchalance which completely captivated me; for how was I to know that the very attributes I admired in this man were born of his intimate experience with women; or, in short, that he appreciated them because he was a voluptuary.

Tolstoi's Kreutzer Sonata.

It is difficult for a person of my temperament to disbelieve in those who please them. The distrust must come through bitter experience, and my disillusion came through matrimony. Even now, when to forget would be a happiness I never hope to realize, does my memory recall in vivid detail every thrill of joy that filled my heart the night I was betrothed to Posdnicheff. I remember just how our boat rocked to and fro as it drifted along in the moonlight, and how he praised the shimmer of my hair, and vowed I was the only woman he had ever loved. I remember, too, that after our marriage, his first allusion to this betrothal night was one of scorn. He said, had it not been for the moonlight on the water, the shimmer of my perfumed hair, and the exquisite fit of my gown, he would fortunately have remained heart-whole. Doubtless he was right, for well do women know that men esteem them in proportion to their physical attractions; and if in addition they have brain combined with a certain degree of docility that renders them governable, why, so much the better. This all women know instinctively, but no pure woman ever dreams of the depth of moral degradation into which she may be plunged by the man who swears to honor and protect her.

"My engagement to Posdnicheff was brief; and my fondness and childlike trust in him rendered sacred every detail of preparation toward that great event, which I told myself should permit me to dwell in the sunshine of his presence as long as life should last. Our courtship, however, was the only pleasant period I was permitted to enjoy with Posdnicheff; and this was destined to be interrupted. I shall never forget the awful moment wherein he temporarily shattered my confidence, and for the time obliterated every vestige of happiness. Had I been less attached to him, or had I been more experienced, when he showed me his diary in which was enough guilt to blast him in the eyes of the world, I would have then renounced him forever; but God pity me! I was a very child in experience, and in my weakness, and young girl's love, I forgave him, compelling myself to believe that his affection for me, had made him a different man, and that he was now a creature incapable of a sin so heinous as that portrayed in his diary by his own confession. Oh, the fallacy, the hallucination of that blind infatuation the world calls love.

"The break in our courtship was patched up, and wedding preparations went on with increased rapidity. But alas! how swift my disillusion. The anticipated honeymoon palled upon my taste, and like the fabled apples of the Dead Sea, turned to ashes. All the mental congeniality and union of soul of which I had dreamed, vanished forever in a tide of aversion and disgust. I found myself wedded to a monster, who viewed my every act with jealousy and suspicion. How well do I remember, when I was no longer able to control my feelings in his presence, I endeavored to evade him by a pretense that I was fretting for my mother; but when he failed to console me, and began chiding me as capricious, I ceased crying and burst into such a state of frenzied rage as to astonish him into quietude. It was our first quarrel, and it was a fierce one. A mighty chasm which neither of us should ever be able to bridge had suddenly yawned between us. Quarrel followed quarrel in rapid succession, each more bitter than the preceding one; and yet, violent as were these quarrels, there were intervals when this man's bitterness and jealousy were for the time being forgotten, only to burst forth with renewed fury. Picture to yourself what to a pure woman such a life must have been! Hell can hold no terror to one who suffered as did I. Posdnicheff's diabolical jealousy seemed continually to increase, until finally no man dared address me upon the most commonplace topic, that his motives were not impugned. He was even jealous of my attentions to my babe — my little Basil, who brought the first gleam of sunshine to my married life. Ere long, however, a baby in the household ceased to be a novelty, and domestic cares crowded upon me with such rapidity that my health became broken and my nerves completely shattered; and I am satisfied, that but for the timely and persistent interposition of my family physician, who insisted that I must have a complete rest, both physical and mental, my miserable existence must surely have had a speedy termination. This was the source of another fierce quarrel between Posdnicheff and myself, he avowing that no rascally doctor had any right to intrude his advice. In this instance, however, I was firm; and after a three months' visit to my paternal home (my first in ten years), so rapid was the improvement in my shattered health and broken spirits, that I returned to my family with almost the buoyancy of youth in my veins. Inevitable burdens were more easily borne, and even the fault-finding and unkindness of Posdnicheff ceased to trouble me. For the first time in years, I took an interest in things that had been my delight in girlhood days. Once more I tirelessly applied myself to the piano, until I again became a first-rate performer. All this, however, was witnessed by Posdnicheff with direct distrust and indignation; but having grown calloused through long abuse, a spirit of complete indifference now took possession of me, or I should have been utterly wretched under his constant and vindictive reproach. Well do I remember his turning away from me one day, muttering: 'Curse her! She is more beautiful than the day I married her;' and I remember, too, just what a revengeful thrill of happiness flashed over me as

I mentally congratulated myself, that I was spared something, which my tyrannical master had been unable to destroy. Affairs went on at this rate for several months, when suddenly there entered upon the scene of my lonely existence the one destined to forever change its tenor. Well do I remember the slightest details connected with my first meeting of Tronkhatchevsky, of whom I had often heard Posdnicheff speak, but had never met, owing to the fact that he had been in Paris since a year previous to my marriage. I remember that I was looking very well the afternoon that Tronkhatchevsky called, and I remember noting the fact with satisfaction after he had gone. Not that I cared to make any particular impression upon him, other than the desire to please, which is the innate characteristic of every woman. I remember, also, my pleased surprise at the cordial invitation Posdnicheff tendered him to return the same evening and bring his violin; and I detected, too, what one less acquainted with Posdnicheff would have failed to do, viz., something other than a desire to enjoy Tronkhatchevsky's company, and his music — an insane desire (born of furious jealousy) to throw his wife into the society of another man, that he might secretly observe her conduct. Tronkhatchevsky was the sort of man all his fellows must admire. Frank, open, and generous to a fault. His face, although delicate, was strong, and his magnetic eyes, and auburn hair which fell artistically across his brow, were the eyes and hair which belong to an intense and highly poetical temperament. Although a genius, he was as particular, in all the little niceties of dress and social custom, as the veriest exquisite might have been. As I now look back upon the first evening spent in his society I wonder at the strange fatality, which at this critical moment impelled Posdnicheff to throw us together. I knew at the expiration of that first evening, that should circumstances permit (as they bid fair to do), this musician must necessarily fill the void in my lonely existence. Not that anything tangible presented itself to my mind, only a sense of real comfort experienced in his presence, a feeling that life must be less lonely for knowing him. Long afterward, I learned that this intuition was mutual with Tronkhatchevsky. Whether or not Posdnicheff read anything of it in the expression of either of our faces, I do not know; but he watched us narrowly the entire evening, and I noted the expressions of jealousy I knew so well contract his countenance. The evening passed more pleasantly to me than any I had spent for years. Tronkhatchevsky's music, played with the spirit of a real artist, and the pleasure of accompaning with the piano a violinist such as he, made the evening an exceedingly enjoyable one to me. At its close, I was somewhat surprised at the intensity of Posdnicheff's assumed cordiality toward Tronkhatchevsky, and his pressing invitation to him to return at his earliest convenience. Weeks rapidly grew to months, and the mutual devotion of Tronkhatchevsky and myself to music, together with the earnest solicitations of Posdnicheff that he should visit us often, threw us frequently in each other's society." Here the nun paused, and once more pressed her hand convulsively to her left side, as though to suppress a sudden pain. Her colorless lips were tightly compressed, and her eyes closed. The priest trembled as he looked at her, so exactly was she the counterpart of a corpse.

CHAPTER III.

TEN minutes elapsed ere the strange visitor resumed her story. "Yes," she continued, "it is useless for me to deny that ere six months passed Tronkhatchevsky was the very sunshine of my existence. In a thousand nameless and unobtrusive ways, he caused me to realize that I was the one woman in all the world to him; and after all, was it other than natural that one so crushed, so abused, so tyrannized over as was I, should reach out after a stray gleam of sunshine that chanced to cross my darkened pathway! In the sight of God, who justly judges His creatures by their motives, there was no sin in this love which was spontaneous, and which I was utterly unable to control." She heaved a deep sigh, and a bitter smile of sarcasm curled her white lips as she exclaimed, "Heaven pity deluded women! for dark as Erebus is the sea of trouble through which they must pass, ere they lose entire faith in that creature so unworthy of it — man. Once more life seemed tinged with the rainbow gleams of bygone days, and time sped on flower-tipped wings, when suddenly, as a storm cloud gathers in a clear summer sky, so the jealousy of Posdnicheff, which had been quietly strengthening, burst, in all its awful fury, upon my unprotected head. Posdnicheff himself had planned for a dinner after which the guests were to be entertained by Tronkhatchevsky's music. With seeming interest and delight, he had busied himself in sending out numerous invitations to his chosen guests, as well as by ordering an elaborate menu, when suddenly, a day or two before this dinner was to take place, I noted a change in him. He was sullen and morose, and I guessed immediately that jealously was the cause of it. He secluded himself in his study, and I decided to go to him, and if it were possible, to conciliate him. I entered the study, and looking toward me without speaking, he lighted a cigarette, and began smoking. Seating myself beside him, I leaned my head against his shoulder, exclaiming, 'Why do you smoke when you see I wish to talk to you?' He recoiled from my touch, with a look of hatred and disgust. 'If you do not wish me to play with Tronkhatchevsky I will not do so,' I continued, 'and all you have to do, is simply to write our invited guests that I am ill.' He burst into a volley of the most horrible oaths, and swore that I had disgraced myself and dishonored him. Fiercely we flung vindictive epithets, until seizing me by the arm, in a terrible voice he roared: 'Go before I kill you.' 'Are you mad?' I cried. His eyes seemed to emit sparks of fire, as with a voice hoarse with rage, he shrieked: 'Go before I kill you,' and seizing a heavy paper weight, he threw it violently at my feet, and as I turned to fly, hurled after me a massive candle-stick, still shouting like a madman: 'Go, I tell you — go before I murder you.'

"I became unconscious, remaining so for hours; I learned afterward, that I laughed and wept alternately during all this period. When I again grew calm, under the influence of connubial love, my husband kissed me and I forgave him. He confessed to me afterward, that he had been jealous of Tronkhatchevsky. He decided, however, that the dinner should go on as planned, lest some one guess the real condition of affairs (as it had been publicly announced that we were to play). I determined, however, to notify Tronkhatchevsky that after this dinner all intercourse between us should cease. The opportunity came to me during a rehearsal which occurred the evening previous to our dinner, and from which, fortunately, Posdnicheff chanced to be absent. God alone knew the anguish it caused me to voluntarily put out of my life the last ray of sunshine that was ever to gladden it. To murder the truest and purest sentiments that ever bless the human soul; to tear myself from a spirit God and nature had so perfectly attuned in every way to my own, and all, that in the eyes of the world I might obey its conventionalities, by remaining loyal to the man who had forever cursed and blighted my life. I shall never forget the expression upon Tronkhatchevsky's handsome face," she continued dreamily, "when

I made known to him the scene which had occurred between Posdnicheff and myself, and which had led to my decision. As a man might plead for his life, so he plead with me to relent, but I remained firm, telling him that upon the morrow we should meet for the last time. The morrow came, and with it our guests. Dinner passed off as dinners usually do, and then followed our music. I seated myself at the piano, a strange pain tugging at my heart. For the last time! for the last time! seemed to ring in my ears like a funeral dirge. I was trembling so violently that I could scarcely arrange the music. I am certain that Posdnicheff noticed my extreme nervousness, which I presume he considered due to my inferior talent, and the difficult accompaniment I was about to perform. Doubtless he also took note of the manner in which the eyes of Tronkhatchevsky and myself were riveted upon each other's face as I began giving the pitch. Tronkhatchevsky was as pale as death, but not a muscle of his face betrayed emotion, and his hand was perfectly steady as he drew the bow across the violin. He leaned toward me for an instant, under the pretense of a suggestion regarding the music. 'Through this music my soul shall commune with yours,' he whispered; and the music we were about to perform was indeed that in which every passion of the human heart is portrayed — for Beethoven, like Shakespeare, is the master delineator of every human passion, and the piece we were about to perform was Beethoven's wonderful Kreutzer Sonata. If ever passion was portrayed in music, if ever one soul communed with another through the divine melody of sound, it was mine with that of Tronkhatchevsky, in his exquisite rendering of the Kreutzer Sonata. My accompaniment was wholly mechanical, for I was completely absorbed in the poem of sweet sound which the man (whom in spite of myself) I so tenderly loved, was pouring into my soul. That first presto movement, ah! I can hear it yet; it is like a great draught of wine, it intoxicates. The very soul of Tronkhatchevsky mingled with that of mine in the sweet waves of melody, now soft and pleading, and anon sobbing with passion. All the music which followed this during the evening could not for an instant efface its impression. It seemed to have exerted an almost hypnotic influence upon me, and the remainder of the evening Tronkhatchevsky's passion for me as expressed in his performance of that wonderful Kreutzer Sonata seemed to envelop me like a garment.

"A strange feeling of desolation came over me, as upon the departure of our last guest, I closed the piano; a dim, half-conscious feeling that in my loneliness I should never care to renew the remembrance of the happy hours with which the piano should ever be associated. Two days dragged wearily by, leaden days, gray with regret, and longings for that which I had voluntarily put out of my life. Days during which I strove with eager nervous energy, to engross myself with the children and household affairs. At the close of these, Posdnicheff suddenly announced that he was about to leave home upon business which was to detain him about a week. His leaving home was always a cause of thanksgiving upon my part, but it was seldom he was detained longer than a couple of days. His absence for a week would have been a source of unbounded satisfaction to me, had I not been bitterly depressed over the giving up of Tronkhatchevsky, toward whom, in spite of all determination otherwise, my obdurate heart would involuntarily turn. The morning of Posdnicheff's departure, there came to me a letter in a familiar hand, the sight of which sent the blood, with a bound, from heart to brain. It was from Tronkhatchevsky, and stated that he had bade Posdnicheff farewell that morning at the station, and that his own plans were arranged for an immediate return to Paris, in all probability never to revisit Russia. Then came a passionate entreaty to meet him once more for a final farewell. The intensity of this man's passion for me was such that each sentence seemed to glow in jewel-like splendor. How long, think you, did my cold philosophical reason struggle in the current of such a passion? My will once so strong, seemed now but a poor wind-tossed reed; and as one starving would eagerly grasp a morsel of food, so I hastened to let this man, for whose presence I would have sacrificed my life, know that on the morrow he might come to me." She paused as if for breath, and her breathing grew difficult and labored, while again she pressed her hand convulsively to her left side, as though she fain would still a pain that was well-nigh unbearable. "Let me hasten over this part of my experience which it almost takes my life to relate," she resumed, her voice hoarse with emotion. "The following evening Tronkhatchevsky came; and as I look back upon that, the last happy evening of my life, I wonder that some premonition did not come to me that I was upon the eve of an awful tragedy. But no — naught save the knowledge that I was soon to part from the man I loved, marred those moments of perfect bliss. Ye gods!" she panted, "how soon it was all over! The evening had flown so rapidly that we failed to note the lateness of the hour, which was something past one o'clock. Tronkhatchevsky and myself had repaired to the dining-room to partake of some refreshments, when suddenly the door opened and we were confronted by Posdnicheff, who, pale as death, stood with hands clasped behind him. Doubtless the countenance of Tronkhatchevsky and myself betrayed a mingled expression of surprise and fear, with perhaps a tinge of displeasure at this sudden interruption. Tronkhatchevsky was the first to break the silence. "We have been practicing some music," he remarked; and then I ventured to exclaim: "You are back sooner than you expected to be." Not a word issued from the white lips of Posdnicheff, as with the fury of a madman he threw himself upon me, endeavoring to secrete from Tronkhatchevsky the dagger which he carried, in order, doubtless, that he might stab me in the throat or heart. But its glitter attracted Tronkhatchevsky's attention, and clutching Posdnicheff's hands, he loudly cried: "What are you doing? Are you mad? Help! help!"

"Never have I seen anything to compare with the hideousness of Posdnicheff's face as he tore his hands from the grasp of Tronkhatchevsky, and threw himself heavily upon him; but the livid face and purple lips, the protruding eyes and glittering dagger never swerved me for an instant from my determined effort to save the man I loved; and hurling myself upon his left arm, I bore down heavily upon him. He strove to throw me off, but I bore more heavily still, giving Tronkhatchevsky an opportunity to escape with his life. Summoning all his strength, Posdnicheff struck me full in the face. With a scream I fell upon the sofa, crying out: 'There is no wrong between us! None! None! I swear it!' My words seemed to increase his fury, for catching me by the throat he shook me so violently as to almost strangle me. With both hands I clung to his, endeavoring to tear them from my throat, when suddenly he buried the dagger in my left side between the lower ribs. My God!" she frantically exclaimed, her small scarred hand pressing against the spot where the fatal dagger had pierced, "there has not been a day, not even an hour, since then, that I have not felt the pain of that dagger's plunge just as I felt it then. I clutched at the dagger with both hands, almost severing my fingers, but could not ward off the blow. However, not satisfied with as he supposed murdering me, he dashed me from the couch to the floor, and planting his foot on my face, left thereupon the accursed mutilation which was forever to mark me a monstrosity — a creature to be shunned by all her fellows. I have a vague recollection at this juncture of the old nurse entering, having been attracted by the noise; then, as a jet of blood burst forth, for a time I knew no more. When I recovered consciousness, the first thing of which I was cognizant was the smell of antiseptics in the room, and the next, that I was lying upon the bed propped up very high with cushions. Just then Posdnicheff entered, and nearing the bedside, stood gazing upon me. At sight of him all the horror of the past scene flashed into my mind, and I remember exclaiming in a weak voice: 'You have killed me, and you shall not have any of my children; they shall go to my sister. I hate you! Oh, how I hate you!' Then I grew very cold and speechless. I knew all that was going on about me, and yet was powerless to speak or move. Fedorovich, my faithful physician, of whom Posdnicheff had ever been so jealous, came to the bedside, and examining my pulse, exclaimed: 'She is dead!' Then came all the hideous preparations of death, even to the placing of my body in a coffin. Great God!

my tongue is powerless to utter all the horror I endured. I even knew when the shadows of twilight began to gather, and my little band of weeping children were led from the room by their old nurse, leaving me alone to the night and the horror of my situation. A few hours elapsed, and I again heard footsteps and the sound of subdued voices. Nearer and nearer they came, until they paused beside my coffin. One was the voice of my old nurse, the other (although somewhat disguised) was the voice which to me there was none other like. 'I came here at the request of Father Lyof, who is too ill to come himself,' the soft, musical voice went on to explain. 'I am the priest from a neighboring village.' The old nurse crossed herself reverently in his presence, and left him, as she supposed, alone with the dead. Gently he lifted the cloths from my bruised, discolored face, and gazed down upon me. 'Great Heavens!' he exclaimed, and started back in surprise. Was I so hideous, then, that even he recoiled from me? was the thought which first suggested itself. He lifted my cold, bandaged hands, stroking them caressingly as he murmured:

'Poor, poor girl! who would have ever dreamed of this? Ah God! gladly I would give my life to recall yours for a single moment.'

"How his touch thrilled me! Little waves of electricity seemed to flash down my frozen veins. He leaned forward and kissed me, and I felt a great tear-drop splash upon my face. This tear-drop of human sympathy, this magnetic caress from the man I adored, seemed to infuse within me a new life. I put forth a tremendous effort, a great sigh escaped my lips, which caused Tronkhatchersky to bend eagerly over the coffin. 'Save me!' I faintly gasped! 'Merciful Heaven!' he exclaimed, 'they are burying her alive!' He lifted my head, and held me for an instant in his strong embrace. 'Thank God that I am in time to rescue you!' he whispered hurriedly. 'But, remember, all depends upon perfect silence on your part. Be strong, darling. In one hour I will return, and then, you are *mine, mine forever!*' How his words echoed and re-echoed throughout my brain! From the depths of Hades I had suddenly been ushered into Heaven. The loathsome coffin, in which the most terrible moments of

"HE LIFTED ME FROM THE COFFIN AS THOUGH I HAD BEEN A CHILD."

my life had been spent, suddenly became a downy couch of sweetest repose. The fear, the horror of it all had vanished; for had it not given to me my lover? To my confused brain I seemed actually to have been dead, so vivid was my remembrance of the awful murder scene, so horribly real the comatose condition from which I was recovering. Once during the absence of Tronkhatchevsky, the old nurse came into the room, and I trembled, lest she detect the loud throbbing of my heart, but no, she simply snuffed the candles, relighted a few others, and went her way again. Just before the arrival of Tronkhatchevsky, every moment seemed an age, all sorts of weird fancies and wild forebodings took possession of me. When he did finally arrive, he entered the room so stealthily that I was not aware of his presence until he stood at my side. 'Courage, dearest!' he whispered. 'A few moments more, and all will be well.' He placed a heavy sack on the floor beside me, and returned almost immediately, bearing another of equal weight. Placing it beside the first, he lifted me from the coffin as though I had been a child, and so quick and deft were his movements that ere I was aware of it, I found myself in a close cab which was in near waiting. I learned afterward that the sacks contained one hundred and thirty pounds of lead, and that Tronkhatchevsky hurriedly placed them in the coffin, taking care to put on the lid, which he screwed tightly down. Having completed his plan, he immediately sought the old nurse, to whom he gave strict charge, that upon no condition whatever was the lid to be removed from the coffin: 'For,' he explained, 'not only is the body beginning to decompose, but it is sacrilegious thus to expose the mutilated countenance of a murdered woman to the gaze of the curious; and when the undertaker arrives upon the morrow, say to him, my good woman, that this is the priest's command.' Reverently crossing herself, the old woman assured the supposed priest that his order should be executed, for to the pious Catholic a priest's slightest wish is not to be disregarded, and hence, relieved of all forebodings upon that score, Tronkhatchevsky sprang lightly into the cab, and drove rapidly away."

CHAPTER IV.

"I no sooner entered the carriage than I became again totally unconscious, and so precarious was my condition that to drive farther than the neighboring village would have been to still more surely endanger my life. Tronkhatchevsky, too, was running a risk, by remaining longer in Russia; and in his priest's garb he cautiously entered a private hospital, where he deposited a sufficient sum to insure me the best treatment, and imposed upon the credulity of the institution to such an extent as to lead them to believe that I was an only sister, who having met with a severe accident, he intrusted to their care during an absence on his part, compelled by most pressing ecclesiastical duties. He also succeeded in so profoundly impressing them in his favor, that they bade him an almost affectionate adieu, tendering him implicit assurance that his most minute directions should be faithfully executed, one of which was to notify him daily of my condition, and should I recover, to send me in the care of a competent nurse to his address in Paris. Never shall I forget my convalescence," she continued, while her eyes took on a far-away expression. "Never shall I forget the impatience with which I waited the letters that came so regularly from Tronkhatchevsky, nor my feverish longing for the day upon which I was to go to him. The past seemed a blank to me. Even my children were forgotten. I was as one resurrected from the dead; a new life, roseate-hued with youthful dreams seemed to stretch itself before me. One of my foibles (perhaps the chief) was pride in my personal appearance; but upon my first discovery that my hands (which were my especial pride) had been scarred and disfigured forever, I immediately set about to discover if fate had dealt more kindly with my face; but a mirror was promptly refused me, and I had only the beauty of my magnificent hair with which to console myself. I was totally ignorant of the fact that not only was my beauty of countenance destroyed, but that I had been rendered positively revolting; and when the truth was first revealed to me, and from the mirror, instead of the pink and white beauty so pleasing to my sight, there stared back at me a hideous, blanched, and disfigured face, I wept for days and nights, refusing to be comforted, lest the awful change lessen the love of him whom I now so madly worshipped. Long, tear-stained letters I wrote to him, letters in which I laid bare all the anguish of my tortured soul, all my fears, and misgivings, and it was not until strong, comforting letters in his own familiar hand were returned to me, that my sorrow was lessened, and once more,— I dared to hope.

"As I look back upon that morning, more than thirty years ago, when I quitted Russia forever, it seems to me a whole lifetime has elapsed. For months, my every thought had been one continued dream of meeting Tronkhatchevsky. In my weakened physical condition, I was as one who had been hypnotized. I seemed to feel and see only through Tronkhatchevsky. My great, absorbing passion for him had deprived me of my personality, woman's chief charm. My love was a morbid, consuming passion, which for the time dwarfed, as it were, my mentality. As I look back upon that miserable, pitiful moment of ecstatic bliss, when in

Paris I was once more reunited to Tronkhatchevsky, every fibre of my body tingles with scorn. It is unnecessary for me to detail our meeting. It would have been the one supreme moment of my life, had there not weighed heavily upon me the fear lest my lover's devotion be lessened through my loss of beauty. I was heavily veiled, and for hours refused every entreaty upon his part to uncover my face. The sound of his soft musical voice thrilled me with foolish ecstasy. I was mad with joy to feel his arms about me once more, to hear him whisper sweet nothings which to me meant everything; to listen to his praise of my voice — my exquisite form; to hear his ardent assurance that no physical change could ever in the least affect his devotion to me, and with his arms close about me to hear him call me his own. His — entirely and completely his — I who had been dead and was now resurrected that I might live again, as it were, in another world. Ah! the mad joy of the moment was too intense to last." She paused, panting for breath; a strange light gleamed in her eyes, which suddenly faded away, giving place to a look of bitter scorn. "Bah!" she continued with a shudder, "why recall all this? But," she slowly added, while a bitter laugh escaped her white lips, "what matters it after all to one whose heart has turned to stone? Swiftly as the approach of a hurricane, happiness gave place to despair. I lifted the veil from my face, and Tronkhatchevsky positively recoiled from my presence. There was a look of horror upon his handsome face, which he was plainly struggling to conceal. He arose with bowed head, his long, white fingers covering his beautiful eyes, and walking slowly across the room, paused at the door. 'Poor maimed darling!' he exclaimed, 'I am totally unprepared for this — I must be alone for a little while.' And with the look of horror upon his face, he unceremoniously left the room. It was the last time I ever beheld him. Swift as an electric stroke was the metamorphosis I underwent. From a loving, trusting woman, I was transformed to a creature whose hatred for man was so fierce as to almost consume my vitality. I tarried not a moment in Paris, but quitted it forever, and coming immediately to England, entered this neighboring convent as a nun, and here for thirty years I have tried in vain to live a life of holiness and peace; tried in vain to conquer my hatred for your sex, sufficiently, at least, to seek absolution through the Confessional; but not until I beheld your life of lowliness and self-sacrifice, could I bring myself to believe that any goodness dwelt in man; and to you, and you only, I felt that I could reveal the history of my shattered life." The sweet passionate voice had ceased its story, and the monk with bowed head conducted her to the Confessional.

"Ego te absolvo a peccatis tuis in nomine Patris, et Felii, et Spiritus Sancti. Amen." His words were broken by sobs, but they brought sweet peace to the tired spirit of the nun. Issuing from the Confessional, the monk exclaimed: "Daughter, since both you and I have forsworn all mortal passion, I would free your heart of its bitterness toward the man who with you has sinned. I would not shield him, for his sin has been greater than yours, and his suffering equal; and yet, you were hasty in your misjudgment of him. He sought you all over Europe, and finding you not, his entire life has been devoted to ministering to others." "Do you know whereof you speak?" asked the nun with a queer tremor in her voice. The monk lifted his head, and the two looked at each other. All traces of age and sorrow in the face of the Benedictine seemed suddenly to have disappeared. True, the hair on his brow was snowy and thin; the long fingers, once so white and shapely, were now hard and worn with toil; the master hand of the artist had lost its cunning; but the beautiful eyes, which in the long ago had found their way into the heart of Posdnicheff's wife were the same. The face, too, at this instant wore its old familiar aspect, save that it was spiritualized, glorified, shining, as it were, with an ethereal light. With a glad cry of recognition the nun sprang to her feet, and the two stood gazing into each other's faces in mute rapture. They were like two spirits of another world, who having undergone the mysteries of life and death, stood calmly looking back upon it all. There was not a vestige of earthly passion in the riveted gaze which so plainly reflected the splendor of their mutual love; and as death ofttimes destroys the lines of age upon a face, and imprints upon the frozen image a smile, so, by some strange revulsion, at this eventful moment the poor scarred face of the nun assumed its old-time beauty. These people, who had suffered so long and so deeply, who loved each other with an exalted passion seldom known to mortals, and who were soon to part forever, stood looking into each other's eyes as though they fain would gaze forever. It was a marriage of soul, and the union was complete. They did not even clasp hands in parting; their love was too high, too exalted, to partake of aught that was earthly. For one brief instant the nun knelt at the feet of the monk for his blessing. "Bendicat vos omnipotens Deus, Pater, et Filius, et Spiritus Sanctus," he slowly repeated. "Amen," came the reverent response; and swiftly and silently the slight, dark-robed figure glided out into the night, and away from his presence forever.

[Reprinted through the courtesy of "Frank Leslie's Popular Monthly."]

ROMANCE OF A KENTUCKIAN
IN ST. AUGUSTINE

CHAPTER I.

THE season at St. Augustine was at its height, and the Ponce de Leon thronged with gay pleasure seekers, with a small scattering of their less fortunate fellows, who hoped in the balmy sea air of the quaint little Spanish city to woo back the fickle goddess, health.

In the spacious dining salon, where each artistic appointment breathes the rich sensuous Renaissance spirit, at a table near one of the great oak pillars supporting the dome sat a man of such Herculean form and beauty of countenance as is found most often among the men of Kentucky. Magnificently proportioned, he carried himself like a god; his regal head was poised upon a full round throat; his gray eyes, changeable with emotion, smiled from beneath a broad low brow, smooth and white as a woman's, and about which clustered rich, slightly curling brown hair, while above a pair of beautiful red lips curled a perfectly kept golden-brown mustache.

This magnificent Adonis of the famous Blue Grass region of Kentucky bore the sensation his appearance always created with the utmost sang-froid. While awaiting his dinner order, although seemingly absorbed in the allegorical illustrations of the stained glass windows opposite him, he nevertheless started perceptibly as a tall, beautiful blonde, together with an elderly woman, entered the dining-room.

Grace Ashmore was a beauty, an heiress, and withal, a heartless coquette, although her friends credited her with at last having surrendered her heart (if she possessed that seemingly unnecessary and unfashionable appendage of the nineteenth century) to the young Kentuckian, who was far handsomer than any of the New Yorkers who had followed the beautiful heiress to the Ponce; moreover, he combined with esprit and faultless manners a certain

in St. Augustine.

warmth and enthusiasm which characterize the men of Kentucky. It was as if he had absorbed something of the sunshine of his native land, something of the beauty and massiveness of its splendid fields and rolling meadows.

From the minstrels' gallery above, sweet music floated down the vast brilliantly lighted dining-room, and as Grace Ashmore quitted it, she seemed in her undulating, serpentine grace a very poem set to the melody of sound. Throwing a light fleecy wrap about her shoulders, she stepped into the outer court with her chaperon, where she was speedily joined by the handsome Kentuckian, George Allen Van Zant.

It was a perfect February night and the tropical splendor of the court brilliant with its brightly colored flowers, its electric fountains, gleaming like strands of rainbow colored gems; its vines from which depended myriads of bright-hued blossoms; its graceful palmettos, and over all its oriental splendor and glowing beauty; the wafted odor of its wilderness of roses, mingled with the faint perfume of the orange grove beyond, made it a very Eden for lovers, even though encumbered by a chaperon. Strolling through the court chatting gaily, the trio came suddenly upon a little crouching figure, whose flowing blue-black tresses were picturesquely crowned with a wreath of scarlet pomegranite blossoms, and whose small daintily poised head was turned sidewise, canary-like, to catch every strain of music with which the orchestra was flooding the Ponce.

"A pretty picture, and well deserving this oriental setting," murmured the chaperon pointing toward the child.

"That is Petronilla Pedro, a little Spanish flower girl who is music mad," replied the Kentuckian.

At the sound of approaching voices the child sprang to her feet, bearing lightly upon her arm a basket of flowers. Recognizing the handsome Kentuckian, who was not only a liberal purchaser of her posies, but whom upon learning the little maiden's passion for music, had promised her lessons of the Cathedral organist, she smilingly approached him and timidly tendered him a beautiful tea-rose.

in St. Augustine.

Touching the little flower-crowned head tenderly he offered her a coin, but she folded her tiny brown hands across her breast, and shaking her head replied: "It is a gift." Thanking her kindly the young man turned towards Grace Ashmore and would have fastened the rose in her wealth of golden hair, but the small Petronilla anticipated his movement, and springing toward him with the ferocity of a young tigress, snatched the rose from his hand, scattered the petals upon the ground, and stamping them under her tiny feet fled rapidly from the court.

"Whew," whistled the nonplussed young man, "my little protégée seems to have misunderstood my attempted reverence for her gift. I wish I could overtake and console her." A peal of merry laughter greeted his remark. "Nonsense, Colonel Van Zant," replied the beautiful Grace, "Do you not see that the little vixen is jealous of me?"

"Jealous!" reiterated the young man incredulously, "Why she is but a baby."

"Yes, jealous," laughed the beauty. "A little Spanish woman in embryo; and I promise you, were she grown up, I would not care to have such a fury cross my pathway. Why the little monster's eyes gleamed vengeance and destruction."

Meanwhile the "Little Monster," as the fair New Yorker termed her, was speeding down the street with throbbing heart and tear-wet eyes. On—on she went, never pausing until she reached the sea wall, where she suddenly stopped, and kneeling down, gazed far out seaward; for to the child, over that vast expanse of water, there seemed ever to linger a sadness, in harmony with her own lonely little life. Suddenly a pair of strong hands lifted the sobbing child to her feet and a kindly voice exclaimed, "Heigho! little girl, are you crying because you couldn't sell your posies?" and thrusting twice the price of the flowers into her hand, he was gone. It was a handsome face that looked down into that of the little flower girl, but it was not the face of George Van Zant, and the sobbing little creature was in no wise comforted; for this small "music mad" Spanish maiden was desperately and passionately in love with the handsome Kentuckian.

CHAPTER II.

THE following day, and indeed for several successive days, did George Van Zant haunt the courts of the Ponce, hoping to meet and conciliate the little creature whose feelings he had so unwittingly outraged. It was not, however, until a week subsequent, when strolling alone in the vicinity of the Old Fort that he chanced across her.

"Roses!—fresh roses!" called the clear treble child voice; and then, finding herself face to face with her hero, rich waves of color rushed to the little olive face, and the great star-like eyes filled with tears.

"Petronilla! what have I done to offend you that you shun me thus?" asked the young man drawing her to him. If you, my reader, could have listened to the music of the man's voice, could have looked upon the beauty of his face, the magnificence of his form, and could have felt the magnetism of his presence, you would not have wondered at the pair of little brown hands which clasped themselves about his neck, and the broken little voice which sobbed out:—

"I love you — and you — you — love her — the woman to whom you would have given my rose," and then withdrawing herself from his embrace, with a quaint touch of dignity, mingled with something of the fierceness which ran riot in her Spanish blood, stamping her little, arched foot like a tragedy queen, she exclaimed: —

"I hate her! I hate her!" "Listen Petronilla, you little untamed wild bird," exclaimed the young man persuasively, "do you not know that the beautiful woman to whom I would have given your rose is my promised wife? and who knows but that she might learn to love you as I do, and then we" ——

"Never! Never!" fiercely interrupted the child. "I hate her. I would murder her," and throwing herself at his feet, she wept as though her very heart would break, and as the young man gazed down upon the agonized little form at his feet, he felt he would have given much to have seen one tithe of the sentiment this child felt for him expressed by the cold beautiful woman who had promised to become his wife. Suddenly, as though she had evolved some revelation, she sprang to her feet, her

"I LOVE YOU, AND YOU — YOU LOVE HER."

in St. Augustine.

dark tear-gemmed eyes sparkling, and seizing both the young man's hands, exclaimed:—

"Seignior, she will never become your wife, never—never; something tells me so. Then when I am quite grown up you will find me, and I will marry you."

Pleased that the child's fancy should be of comfort to her, he replied:—

"Yes, Petronilla, if my promised wife proves me false, I will never marry unless I marry you; and now, as I go away to-morrow, what shall I give my little sweetheart by which to remember me most pleasantly?"

"A ring, Seignior," replied the child gravely, "I will wear it until you come for me."

The pretty turquoise ring which the young man bought and placed upon the finger of his devoted little protégée was not his only gift to her. The Cathedral organist received a year's tuition, with instructions to teach the "music mad" little maiden to sing; and when, two years later, the little girl's pure, beautiful soprano rang out through the old Cathedral, as clear and as sweet as a trill from the mocking birds she loved to imitate, so entranced with her voice became a wealthy Englishwoman that she carried the little Southern song-bird back to her English home, there to give her the advantages of which she must have otherwise been deprived.

CHAPTER III.

THE Opera House at Lexington (fairest city of all the fair ones in the grand old State of Kentucky) was filled to overflowing with an audience eager to hear the new songstress, who had taken Europe by storm and who upon coming to New York had sung to crowded and enthusiastic audiences for a week, when she suddenly and capriciously threw up her engagement, declaring that she would make a tour of Kentucky at once, or return to Europe; and her long-suffering manager, driven to desperation through the fear of losing her, had been compelled to accept her conditions.

The rising curtain revealed to the eager Kentucky audience the slight, beautiful, rounded figure of a young girl whose delicate oval face

"THE SLIGHT, BEAUTIFULLY ROUNDED FIGURE OF A YOUNG GIRL."

seemed almost child-like, and whose dark velvet eyes glanced inquiringly over the audience, as though seeking some familiar face. Suddenly her eyes rested upon a figure kingly in its magnificence, and crowned with the head and face of an Adonis; rested long and earnestly, as though fain to rest there forever. The entire audience watched the prima donna with intense admiration (with the exception of the one man upon whom she gazed as though fascinated, and unable to turn away). Suddenly he looked at her, but in his great luminous eyes there was not the slightest gleam of recognition, nor even of interest; he glanced at her coldly and turned away. Every vestige of color faded from the girl's face. She stood before her audience colorless as a bit of sculptured marble. The orchestra had ended its prelude and was waiting for her. It recalled her to herself, and the voice which fell upon the ears of the listening audience thrilled with such rich, passionate pathos, such tender, plaintive appeal that there were many tear-wet eyes when the curtain fell.

"Quick," demanded the prima donna of an attendant (while the orchestra played between the acts), "bring here the Opera House manager until I speak to him." Her command was no sooner spoken than obeyed.

"At your service," exclaimed the manager of the Opera House, bowing low.

"Tell me, quick!" exclaimed the girl imperiously, "The man in the box, to the right, is it George Van Zant?"

"It is Colonel Van Zant, Miss," was the reply. "He is an old-time friend of mine," she replied, "tell me of him, is he married?"

"Married? No!" answered the manager. "He was to have married a beautiful New Yorker, they say, but about ten years ago a spell of illness left him totally and incurably blind, and the girl refused to marry him. Shall I send him your card, Miss?"

"No, not for the world," answered the girl waving his dismissal; and this time there was a thrill of such unmistakable pleasure in her voice that the man wondered at it, thinking to himself, that "foreigners were a queer lot any way."

The curtain arose for the second act, and the audience bent forward in pleased surprise at the

in St. Augustine.

radiant creature who appeared before them, her cheeks glowing, her great star-like eyes shining with happy excitement — and her voice — (could it be the same to which they had listened a few moments before?) soared in a wonderful burst of glad melody, until her listeners asked themselves if the singer were not more than mortal — and wondered, too, what had wrought in the capricious songstress such change. Surely, child-like, although she seemed, she could not have been intimidated, for had she not sung before the crowned heads of Europe? No, they told themselves, she was simply as great an actress as singer, and wooed her hearers to laughter, or tears, at her will. Sweeter, fuller, clearer, soared the beautiful voice, replete with joyous melody. The audience was breathless with delight, and the soul of the blind man, for whom, all unknown, was poured out this flood of melody, reveled in its beauty. The beautiful sightless eyes of the blind Adonis smiled, even as they had done in the long ago; and to the song queen, upon whose voice the listening people hung entranced, that smile brought the same rapture that it did ten years ago to the little Spanish flower girl, whose sunshine it was, and from whose memory it had never been effaced.

CHAPTER IV.

It was one of those perfect days found only in June; and a June day in central Kentucky is the embodiment of all that is beautiful in nature, a bouquet of her fairest culling, a rhapsody-flower scented and roseate-hued, set to the melody of singing birds, and whispering zephyr-kissed leaves. Such was the day following the evening of the great prima donna's appearance in Lexington, and when that capricious little bohemian ordered her driver to stop the carriage a quarter of a mile the other side of Colonel Van Zant's residence and await her return, it created no surprise, such as similar conduct upon the part of a well-regulated young lady would have caused.

The girl paused and drew a long breath, as though fain to drink in some of the beauty and freshness about her. The sun was golden in the clear azure of the heavens, and through the grand old forest trees, it sifted a shower of amber gems, which gleamed upon the mossy turf beneath. Leaves stirred lazily in the warm perfumed air, and birds sang far and near, as though in compliment to the sweet singer who listened to them, while about her on every side spread fields and meadows, in all the broad rolling magnificence which marks the blue grass region of Kentucky. She proceeded slowly towards the grounds surrounding the Colonel's home. It was not unlike most Kentucky suburban homes, spacious, old-fashioned, and almost hidden from the roadside view by the gigantic oaks, which were a prominent feature of the fine old park in which it stood. Having entered the grounds she stopped suddenly, for upon a rustic bench beneath a canopy of trees, his hands folded, his beautiful sightless eyes gazing upon vacancy, sat Colonel Van Zant. Trembling she softly approached and stood silently looking at him. Tears rained down her cheeks as she gazed upon the strong man, helpless as a little child. She drew nearer, and took his hand.

"Mr. George — Colonel Van Zant.". He arose, smiling and surprised. "You do not know me, you did not know you were listening last night to your little 'music mad' Petronilla Pedro?" A pleased expression of surprise mantled his face, and he cordially clasped both of the little singer's hands in his own as he seated her beside him.

"Petronilla! my child," he said, "this is a pleasure I never anticipated. Years ago I wrote to St. Augustine, but could not trace your whereabouts."

"Then you had not forgotten me," exclaimed the girl eagerly.

"Forgotten you! no indeed," he replied, "but how should I know that the great prima donna who had turned half the heads in Europe was my baby sweetheart of St. Augustine; and now, my child, tell me all about yourself, what you are doing, and where you are going."

How lightly he speaks, thought the girl, and never refers to his own great misfortune. "I came to this country, not for laurels, or money, but — but because — I wanted to find you, Mr. George," she answered simply.

"Ah!" he replied, "my little Petronilla imagines herself indebted to me, because I first placed her upon the road to success, and how wonderfully she has compensated me, leaving me the debtor after the rare feast of last night." Great tears welled up in the velvety brown eyes, and throwing her arms about his neck, in utter childlike abandonment, she sobbed:—

"O Mr. George — will you never understand — I came because — because — I love you — and because I want never to leave you."

"Dear little Petronilla," he answered, "I could never accept such a sacrifice." Could the blind man have seen the worshipful passion which radiated the glowing face and beamed from the starlike eyes of this child of nature, he would not have felt her love to be a sacrifice; but alas — he only felt the deep affliction, the mighty gulf which he could not expect woman's love to ever bridge. Suddenly the little hands unclasped themselves from about his neck, and, with a certain touch of dignity, the girl exclaimed:—

"I deserve rebuke, in that I have disregarded the restriction society places upon my sex. I have betrayed to you my love, forgetting that yours was given to another long years ago."

"Petronilla!"—the hands of the blind man groped aimlessly until they touched the little, trembling arm of the sobbing girl, and drawing her within his embrace, he exclaimed, "Petronilla, for God's sake, my darling, do not misunderstand me. When this terrible affliction came upon me, and I found the woman who had promised to become my wife had deserted me, I longed for you, child though you were, as only a man can long for the one thing in life left for him to love, and as I compared your ardent love for me with that of the woman whom your childish prophecy declared should never become my wife, it was as a ray of sunshine beside a miserable, flickering taper. I searched for you, but in vain; and now—now that you are here, in the radiance of your young beauty, and the glory of your magnificent matchless voice, here, with the world in adoration at your feet, can you not feel with me, my darling, the presumption it would be for a helpless, blind man to accept the priceless treasure of your love?"

Very slowly she spoke to him now, and with her arms close about his neck once more, and

in St. Augustine.

the glory of her splendid love illuminating her countenance. "I only know," she said, "that ever since I looked upon your face, ten years ago, I have loved you, nay, worshipped you madly. I only know that I can never love another, having loved you; and that to-day I would gladly exchange the position I occupy for that of the homeless flower girl, if thereby I might be permitted to become your servant."

Very softly and reverently the blind Adonis made reply, as he held the happy girl in his arms:—

"Petronilla, my precious wife, in depriving me of my sight, God has given me a far more priceless jewel."

Let us draw the leafy canopy, beneath which the happy lovers rested, close about them, and intrude no farther upon the sacredness which belongs to perfect love.

The speedy marriage of Colonel Van Zant to the great prima donna gave rise to much comment and many theories. Some said the Colonel had educated her, that he might selfishly appropriate her to himself, when her success was at its zenith; while others declared her a designing creature, who married Colonel Van Zant for a name. Suffice it to say, that in all Kentucky there is not a happier couple than George Van Zant and his beautiful wife, who proudly bears upon her jeweled hand a certain little turquoise ring with which she says the Colonel presented her when a baby, as her engagement ring.

[Reprinted through the courtesy of Frank Leslie's "Popular Monthly Magazine."]

LITTLE JEAN'S THEFT

● ● ●

HE looked so out of place among those debauched criminals, as he stood — a forlorn tiny midget in the New York Police Court. One by one the motley crew pressed forward and received their sentence. Women, whose painted, shameless faces bore not a trace of purity or womanhood; and men, from whose visage one turned and shuddered, wondering if they ever bore the stamp of childhood's innocence.

The Judge turned to the lad. How pinched and small he was. A mop of tangled, yellow curls formed a sort of halo about the little white face, and dark rings encircled the clear blue eyes. With the great toe of his little bare foot he formed circles on the dusty floor, as is the wont of children when in shame.

Little Jean's Theft.

"Look up, my boy!" the Judge exclaimed. "Yours is a curious theft, this stealing flowers, and I am told this is your third offense. Now had you stolen that to eat, t'would not have seemed so strange, but flowers, always flowers. Now tell me, lad, what it is tempts you thus to steal these flowers, and from a stall where fruit and candy lay within your reach."

The boy looked up. Great tear-drops trickled down his worn white cheeks, which bore traces of the grimy little hands that brushed them off.

"Please, sir," he made reply, "before I came to live in this great town, where all the streets are brick, I lived alone with mother and our flowers. But she was sick, and all the time she coughed, and white and thinner grew, and one day, sir,—the last before she died,—she took some flowers, and giving them to me, said: 'Little Jean, whenever you see flowers, think of me;' and, sir—I live up many flights of steps, quite near the sky—and when I have a flower, *I'm up so high*, I'm sure she sees, and smiles to know I think of her; and when I hold the flower and go to sleep, my mother always comes and kisses me."

Little Jean's Theft.

The Judge's cheeks were wet with tears.

"God bless you, boy," he said, "as sweet a flower as you, my child, shall not fade for want of tender care."

The child had found a protector; yet still, as the cherished pet of a happy home, his sweetest joy is to gather flowers, and show the angel mother that "Little Jean" still thinks of her.

NUMBER FOURTEEN

* * *

IN A Mott Street tenement house in New York, where the air is heavy with that combined polution peculiar only to the over-crowded hovels of poverty, there recently occurred a scene witnessed alone by the Omnipotent. Stretched upon a miserable cot, an emaciated lad of twelve years lay dying. Beside him knelt a weeping woman, who clasped the small cold hands with an anguish known only to mothers. The two were alone, when there suddenly appeared upon the scene a man,—one whose hair was prematurely white, and whose gaunt, trembling form was bowed, but not with age. Ten years had elapsed since the man beheld his family, and this was his first homecoming. He stood, riveted, as it were, to the

Number Fourteen.

spot, unable either to speak or move. His mind wandered feebly back to the halcyon days of childhood. The merry laughter of the now grief-stricken woman before him seemed to re-echo over the awful lapse of years, carrying with it something of the smell of wild flowers, the tangle of bushes and woodland paths, as hand in hand they trudged to and from the country school. Like the varied scenes of a panorama, the man's dreams continued to spread themselves in vivid coloring upon the faded canvas of his memory. Now he was an errand boy, in the great Metropolis which had borne witness to the tragedy of his life. Through long years each faithfully performed duty, tinged with the rainbow hue of hope, seemed bringing him nearer the goal he sought; and the boy, entering young manhood, graced the fair castle of his dreams with her whom from earliest childhood he called his "wee wifie." Still, the gaunt, gray-haired man stood lost in retrospection. Now the bright errand boy had become the trusted private secretary of Lloyd Hutchings, his wealthy employer. Through this maze of bygone years in which

Number Fourteen.

the man was lost, the grief-stricken woman before him was ever the central figure. But her voice had the joyousness of the birds to which they listened in childhood. Again, she was his bride, and he lived over the four brief years of their wedded bliss; the happiest years either had ever known, for both had been orphaned at an early age, and knew no love, save that of each other. There is a blissful economy in nature, whereby a man isolated from his fellows lives almost entirely in the past; blissful, albeit the past is dark, for it is the only preservation from inevitable madness. So this gray-haired man, who had lived apart from his fellows for ten years, stood groping with the past, while the real tragedy of life was transpiring before him. Again he was seated at his employer's desk; he could see the blot upon his book, caused by the sudden placing of a man's hand upon his arm. A soft, treacherous hand; better far had it stabbed him to the heart, than have lingered upon his arm so caressingly. Again he hears the voice of his employer's son, as placing a forged check in his hands (bearing his father's

Number Fourteen.

signature), he bids him cash it, as the hour is late, and other immediate duties call for his attention.

Credulous victim, how promptly he obeyed. Again he lived over the week intervening between the discovery of the forgery; and now he was confronting young Hutchings, only to find an emphatic denial of his participation in the affair. Again — with a dignity borne of innocence, he plead with his employer to believe him; but in vain. His brain swam, as he seemed to see a crowded court-room, and listened to the evidence which was but too true, that he, Harold Hastings, had forged the check. Then came the verdict with its ten years' imprisonment. Life had stopped for him, with the utterance of those few words. The business world shook its head *en masse*, and showered unbounded sympathy upon the martyr head of the opulent employer; but what heed gave it to him, whose individuality had suddenly been merged into that of the machine which justice recognizes only by a number, and who was soon to be forgotten by all save the "wee wifie," who tearfully hugged her baby to her frail bosom, and bravely took up the burden of life alone. Only once, during all those years, were one of her letters given him, and he knew from its tenor that she had written often. It was a brave, strong letter,— one calculated to inspire hope,—with never a word of hardships borne, or labor performed by the frail little hands. Only a great outpouring of love, and a looking forward to his return when they should begin life over again; with here and there a description of little Harold growing ever more like her absent dear one. What pen can portray the awful change wrought in man by solitary confinement! So accustomed had this wretched man become to the once hated appellation of "Number Fourteen," that when upon his dismissal the warden repeated his name, its unaccustomed sound startled him. It was some days after his dismissal until he was enabled to find the miserable abode which gave shelter to his family; and now he stood in their presence, trembling, awed, unable either to speak or move, gazing upon this last sad scene in the drama of his life, as like a panorama its past had flitted swiftly before him. He passed his

Number Fourteen.

hands across his eyes, as one in a dream. Could this emaciated, sad-faced woman, who hung in such anguish over the dying boy, be his beautiful girlish "wee wifie" of ten years ago? He made an effort to move towards her. A long, quivering sigh escaped the lips of the boy, and without a struggle, he closed his blue eyes, never to open them again. "So He giveth His beloved sleep," whispered the mother. "Good-bye, little Harold; you have left mother to wait alone."

The trembling gray-haired man was beside them now, and his voice was broken by sobs, as he exclaimed: "No — wee wifie — the watching is over now." It was indeed, for the faithful spirit of the ex-convict's "wee wifie" had followed that of their child, and it was the marble face of the dead upon which he rained his impassioned kisses. All night long he watched beside his dead, clasping them in his arms, kissing their mute lips, and whispering in their silent ears something of the boundless love with which his poor broken heart was overflowing; but when the morning light struggled in through the narrow casement, he drew

Number Fourteen.

down the ragged blind, and crept softly out into the broad sunlight and away from the putrid air of the crowded alley, where lay all that was dear to him on earth. It was Sabbath morning, and groups of gayly-dressed people were seeking their various places of worship. On through the crowded thoroughfare, the solitary ex-convict wended his way, pausing only at the door of one of the prominent churches. How often, with his wee wifie, he had entered those sacred portals — the last time carrying baby Harold thither to be christened. "Ah, God!" he moaned, and stifled back the sobs which refused to be controled. Too broken hearted was he to note the cold stares the fashionable congregation bestowed upon him, as he crept up the aisle, to the pew he had occupied ten years before. He did not even realize that an usher had hastily led him back; giving to the forward, uncouth stranger a seat nearest the door. "Bear ye one another's burdens." These were the words of the text. Beautiful words they were, but words which the great busy world, and most of all, a fashionable congregation, have little time to

Number Fourteen.

consider. The stranger, in the coarse ill-fitting garb, who wept softly during the eloquent sermon of the popular divine, seemed strangely out of place.

> "Blessed be the tie that binds
> Our hearts in Christian love."

How sweetly the words floated upon the air, borne in waves of song by the cultivated voices of Dr. E's. aristocratic congregation.

> "We share our mutual woes,
> Our mutual burdens bear,
> And often for each other flows
> The sympathizing tear."

As the beautiful soulful words welled forth from the lips of the great congregation, they carried a ray of comfort to the poor bleeding heart of the ex-convict, and inspired him with fresh courage to solicit the favor which had prompted his coming. The moment was at hand. The benediction had been pronounced, and as the congregation thronged the aisle the ex-convict shrinkingly pressed forward to the eloquent divine whose gracious words had strangely soothed his aching heart. Hastily and very pathetically he related his sad story, and concluded

Number Fourteen.

by exclaiming: "I ask you, dear sir, for the sake of her who was once a member of your church, and for the sake of the dead boy, upon whose baby head you lay your hands in the sacred rite of baptism; for their dear sakes, I implore you, give them a Christian burial, and save them from a pauper's grave." The soft voice of the eloquent divine was full of patronization as he replied: "Really, my poor man, this is very sad; but my time is too thoroughly engrossed with my immediate congregation to burden myself with outside affairs. We are taught in God's Word that the way of the transgressor is hard, and I trust past transgressions may save you from future sin." Fiercely the ex-convict turned from the Rev. Dr. ——, and into his face there crept a look which it is well comes not often to the face of man. An hour later, as the eloquent divine was seated at his bounteous board discussing with his cultured family a sermon he had in view, which he trusted would be fruitful in securing large donations toward certain foreign missions in which he was interested, another scene was being enacted in a remote part of the city. A motley crew, such as

Number Fourteen.

the crowded tenement house of a great city alone can reveal, were thronging garret and stairway, called thither by the sharp report of a pistol. Upon a cot, side by side, lay a mother and child, their dead faces wearing a strange look of serenity. Upon the floor beside them, face downward, lay a man with a pistol shot through his brain. A stalwart Irishman pushed through the crowd, and lifting the body from the floor, placed it upon the cot beside the others. Suddenly he started back, and roughly brushing the tears from his eyes, exclaimed:—

"My God!" *It is number fourteen.*"

CATHERINE

A Tale from Real Life.

CHAPTER I.

Surely whoever speaks to me in the right voice, him or her I shall follow,
As the water follows the moon, silently with fluid steps, anywhere around the globe. —*Walt Whitman.*

Softly, through a canopy of glossy leaves and creamy magnolia blossoms, crept the fair June sunshine, flecking with gold the rough brown locks of a girl, who with bowed head, softly wept. Catherine Scharger was the daughter of the most miserly, domineering man in the State of Alabama,—a German, who, settling in the pretty, picturesque town of Selma, had married one of its daughters because of her thrift and industry. But the soft-voiced Southern girl, although inured to the hardships of poverty, had blossomed in that atmosphere of kindly sympathy which to the Southerner is the heritage alike of rich and poor; and after one brief year of cruelty and unkindness, the poor toil-worn hands were folded forever from their labor, and the weary eyes closed, never to open again. Hence, Catherine had never known a mother's love. Before six months her father married again; married a girl as phlegmatic and unsympathetic as himself, and Catherine (Heaven pity her!) had grown to womanhood with never the remembrance of a kiss, a caress, or a kindly word. With her father's stalwart form and blue eyes, she had inherited her mother's tender heart; and this fair June morning, when all nature seemed to unite in one grand symphony of praise, the poor heartsick girl had crept to this secluded spot that she might weep unobserved.

"Hello, Catherine! is you a-cryin'?"

The speaker, Tom Headly, was a short, thick-set fellow, with a coarse face, sensual mouth, and a cast in one eye. Although he had resided in Selma for six months, no one knew from whence he came.

Catherine, vexed to find her solitude broken, ventured no reply.

"I is got somep'n to tell ye, Catherine, ye hear?" he continued.

Catherine lifted her tear-stained face and looked at him sullenly.

"I is going way to-night, an' I'd like to take you with me. I is goin' so far nobody'll ever hear tell of we all. Is you willin' to go, Catherine?"

Still the girl gazed at him sullenly, without reply.

"We all 'u'd live together, Catherine, an' you could keep house. I'd be powerful good to you, girl, an' you might have everything your own way. Is you willin' to go' long?"

He laid his heavy hand caressingly upon the rough brown head. Ah! never was there magician's wand that could vie with the touch of human sympathy; and in all the twenty-four years of her life, this was the girl's first caress.

She lifted her coarse, labor-stained hand, and placing it within Tom's, replied:—

"Reckon I is willin' to go with you, Tom."

Tom leaned forward, and kissed her upon the lips. It was her first kiss, and it was the opening of a new life.

Ah! the rapture of love, to this tender, passionate, starved heart. The honest blue eyes, still moist with tears, shone like violets gemmed with dew, and rich waves of color came and went across the sun-browned face. How fair life seemed now! How gratefully came the faint sweet odor of the jasmine, mingled with the fresher smell of tree and shrub. A mocking bird soaring aloft sent its rich flood of melody athwart the clear azure of the Southern sky. Tiny shafts of sunshine pierced the fragrant canopy above her head, and sent a shower of shadows gleaming at her feet. Catherine felt all this just as the crowd is thrilled by the beauty of a great painting, without comprehension of its artistic conception.

Suddenly a hateful, familiar sound cleft the clear summer air: —

"Cot—o—ree—na!"

It was the voice of her stepmother, and with the agility of a startled fawn the girl bounded to her feet and was gone.

Catherine.

CHAPTER II.

<small>ONE day still fierce, 'mid many a day
struck calm. — *Browning*.</small>

IN a village in southern Ohio stands a log cabin, just as it stood over fifty years ago, when built by Tom Headly; and to the able-bodied, loving-hearted Catherine, whom he installed as its mistress, what a paradise it seemed. How light hearted the once melancholy and morose girl became; for who under the sweet influence of love could be otherwise, be it my lady in her palace, or her servant in the kitchen? It was one stormy night in the month of November following her elopement that the poor girl's happiness (too brief to have dispelled any of its illusions) was brought suddenly to a close. Were this tale an imaginary one, the happiness of its heroine should have been prolonged; but alas! it is only a chapter from the book of life, and where in fiction can be found sorrows so deep, tragedies so thrilling, or love so true and tender, as in real life? In a low chair Tom's hands had fashioned for her particular use,

Catherine.

Catherine sat in the ruddy glow of an open firelight, dreaming, just as myriads of women have, and will ever continue to do. Dreaming of the God-given mystery reserved for woman alone to solve, the beautiful, sacred mystery of motherhood which crowns the lowliest of her sex a queen, as royally as did the immaculate conception of the Mother of God, crown her queen among women. Dream, did our poor Catherine, while her busy fingers deftly shaped wonderful little garments; dream, and smile, in her homely, humble way, glancing now and then proudly at Tom, whose shock of red hair was bent over his work, for Tom was a good carpenter, and this new neighborhood was not slow in recognizing his handiwork. Suddenly the cabin door swung noiselessly open and a tall man, wearing a long white beard, softly entered, and approaching the busy carpenter, gazed down upon him without speaking. Tom glanced up with a gesture of displeasure, gruffly exclaiming: —

"Wal! what does you want, Stranger?"

"What do I want?" returned the man. There was something in the voice which caused Tom

Catherine.

to start violently to his feet and turn deadly pale.

"So you know me, do you?" laughed the man; and dashing aside the disguising beard, with a quick movement he covered Headly with a pistol, at the same time exclaiming:—

"I'll tell you what I want, Tom Headly. I want to avenge my brother's murder; I want your life."

Before the wretched man had time to plead for mercy, he fell at the feet of his avenger, a bleeding corpse.

Six months later Tom Headly's son was born. The shock the mother received had left its impress upon the plastic brain of the child; the boy was simple-minded.

CHAPTER III.

> A solemn thing it is to me,
>   To look upon a babe that sleeps—
> Wearing in its spirit deep
>   The undeveloped mystery
> Of its Adam's taint and woe,
>   Which when they developed be,
> Will not let it slumber so.
> — *Mrs. Browning.*

PREVIOUS to the birth of her child, Catherine remained in a sort of dumb stupor, and it was not until her baby was placed within her arms, that she became aroused to consciousness; and then it was that the poor, starved heart poured out its idolatrous flood of mother love, upon "Tom's baby," as she was wont to call it. Nature is a kind parent, and Catherine, in failing to ever perfectly recover her perceptive faculties, was thus spared the pain of realizing that her child's mind was blighted. To her, "Tom's baby" was all that is bright and beautiful, and in it she "lived, and moved, and had her being." Its tiny arms about her neck, the touch of its rosy fingers upon her face, and the cooing of its baby voice, were manna to

Catherine.

her weary soul. The poor creature was deft at needle work, and tirelessly and unceasingly she labored to support "Tom's baby," and when this self-same baby grew to a strong-limbed lad who developed a taste for tools, and bent over his work with his father's self-same shock of red curling hair, Catherine's delight knew no bounds. For years her simple homely happiness was without alloy, but alas — "the trail of the serpent is over all," and the poor life so replete with suffering was never more to know surcease from its sorrow. Young Tom Headly began frequenting the village alehouses, and ere long, every farthing of his earnings were deposited therein. It is useless to follow poor Catherine through long years of watching and waiting for the coming of unsteady footsteps, the sound of which had once been such music to her ears. Suffice it to say, that her love never faltered, and when old age whitened her head and stiffened her limbs, she still labored to support the son, whose pleasure it should have been to smooth the roughened pathway of her declining years. Eight miles from the village where Catherine resided with her

Catherine.

inebriate son, stood a number of farms, and adjoining one of these a cabin occupied by a family named Taylor, who were distantly related to Tom's father. To this family, "Silly Tom" (as he was commonly called) paid his respects several times a year, always proceeding from thence to Lawrence, there to haunt its more pretentious saloons. It was in one of these that Tom was arrested upon suspicion of having cruelly murdered the entire Taylor family, with the exception of a babe, the pitiful cries of which, as it wandered about in a nude condition, attracted the attention of a distant laborer, who carrying it into the cabin was greeted by the ghastly spectacle of the murdered family. Suspicion immediately attached itself to Headly, whom the neighbors said invariably proceeded to Lawrence after a visit to the Taylors. Upon the day subsequent to the arrest, spots of blood were found upon his shirt and wristbands. He accounted for them by stating that he had butchered hogs the day previous, and to the end stoutly declared his innocence, insisting that he had not visited the Taylors for months. Intense excitement prevailed, and the cry for Headly's blood was such that a riot was feared. The day following the arrest there might have been seen an aged woman creeping along the dusty highway, upon her white head the July sun blazed mercilessly. During her long eight miles' journey to Lawrence she stopped each passerby and gazing wildly and beseechingly into the faces of all she met, exclaimed: "My Tom never did that awful deed." Her coarse shoes were white with dust, her brown and wrinkled face beaded with perspiration, when she reached Lawrence and wended her way to the home of Judge B—, one of the most prominent attorneys. She carried a bucket of berries, which she tendered the lawyer with the simplicity of a child, exclaiming:—

"I gathered them for you; I am Tom's mother. He never did that awful deed, he was too tender hearted to ever kill a bird. I have no money, but, oh God! I must save Tom. You will save my poor boy for me, won't you?"

There was something touching beyond expression in the dumb, tearless agony of the wretched, half-crazed old woman who plead for her son — that son, who to her was still "Tom's baby," the same wee darling she had nestled to her bosom and tended so lovingly. Her appeal was effective; Judge B— being a man of deep feeling and tender heart, responded to the request by a promise of assistance. Several times a week during the interval previous to the trial, the aged woman plodded wearily to Lawrence and presenting herself to Judge B— besieged him with childish and tiresome queries, never forgetting her thank-offering in fruit or vegetables. The tall gaunt figure of the old woman, who wildly asserted to every passerby that "Tom never did that awful deed," became to the citizens of Lawrence a familiar spectacle. The multitude laughed at her as crazy, while a few, realizing that the burden of her cry was but a wail which found its echo in the hopelessness of her own broken heart, pitied her.

Catherine.

Be slow to judge, for mercy given then
Will merit you the same from other men.
—*L. M. Norwood.*

CHAPTER IV.

It was a sultry August morning; and, as if to add to its discomfort, a slight drizzly rain was falling, which intensified the heat. This was the closing day of the great murder trial, which for the past week had kept Lawrence and indeed half the country in an uproar of excitement.

Shortly after sunrise, a motley crowd began assembling about the courthouse, gathering in force as the hour set for the trial approached. Moving slowly toward them, her coarse shoes heavy with mud, her faded frock damp and bedraggled, came the aged mother. She seemed feeble and exhausted, and pausing midst the crowd, gazed wildly into the cold, unsympathetic faces about her, exclaiming: "My poor Tom never did that awful deed; my tender-hearted boy, who never even killed a bird."

A chorus of brutal laughter greeted the appeal, and a coarse creature cried out: "Give us a rest, old woman." A second chorus of brutal laughter greeted this sally, and the old woman (notwithstanding the sultriness of the morning) shivered as if from cold.

The courtroom was crowded to overflowing; not a loophole of escape seemed left the unfortunate defendant. There were blood-spots upon his clothing; the footprints in the soft clay about the door of the murdered family corresponded to a nicety with the size of his shoes; and yet his attorney retained implicit belief in his innocence, and as he arose to deliver his parting address to the jury (upon whose decision hung the life of the prisoner), his voice thrilled with enthusiasm, and his countenance seemed to emit something of the convictions which he so deeply felt. Four long hours he spoke, and never had a speech of such burning eloquence been delivered in the courtroom of Lawrence. He was pleading for a life, that his honest convictions told him was about to be sacrificed instead of one upon whom the awful crime of murder really rested. He spoke of the cornfield surrounding that portion of the cabin in which the murdered bodies lay, and of a man who had been employed in plowing it the entire day of the early evening upon which the murder had been discovered. Proved, too, that he had plowed up to the very window of the room in which the bodies lay and which he must necessarily have seen. He spoke also of the peculiarity of this plowman's failing to hear the piteous cries of the Taylor babe, which were such as to attract the attention of a distant laborer; and of his sudden and mysterious disappearance upon the discovery of the bodies.

Judge B— succeeded in creating well-founded doubt as to the guilt of his client, both in the minds of the jury and the furious outside element. Through the honest convictions and earnest enthusiasm of his attorney, Tom Headly was saved from the gallows; but circumstantial evidence and popular prejudice were such as to render imprisonment for life inevitable.

Who, through the cold medium of pen and ink, would presume to portray the anguish of the poor old mother's farewell? What, though to the world the hands of this half-witted inebriate were steeped in the blood of his fellowmen, was he not to the mother the same babe she had lulled to sleep upon her bosom? The little Tom, whose childish ways had once gladdened her lonely life? Ah! the height, the depth, the breadth of a mother's love! Who can fathom it?

CHAPTER V.

> For the early dead we may bow the head,
> And strike the breast and weep;
> But oh, what shall be said
> For the living sorrow?

EARLY one morning in the latter part of August, there might have been seen slowly wending its way up the main street of a little inland village in Indiana, an ox-cart laden with sundry small household effects, and driven by an aged woman. Any innovation in the way of "a new comer" to this village was a sensation worthy of much observation and comment; and this particular morning, from the residences of my ladies, the lawyer's and doctor's wives, down to those of "the butcher, the baker, the candlestick maker," various heads might have been seen thrust from their several windows, all bent upon observation.

Catherine.

In this particular village there stood an old cabin in which once upon a time there lived a man who murdered his wife and afterwards took his own life, and this cabin the entire community pronounced "hanted," and therefore a place to be shunned by all self-respecting individuals. Why, scarcely a week after the murder, the owner of the cabin having spent a day repairing it, sickened and died mysteriously that self-same night; and barely a fortnight afterward his son fell from the cabin roof and broke his arm. It was enough, then, to arouse suspicion in the virtuous breasts of the horrified villagers, when this new-comer, scorning the advice of the entire community, ensconced herself therein. For a month after her arrival this "brazen-faced old woman" (as the villagers one and all termed her) was discussed with great gusto at all the missionary meetings; although none of the good sisters could surmise why the wretched old creature had brought an ancient crib and a bundle of baby clothes with her.

"Sich a forebodin' lookin' old creetor, too," the barber's wife had remarked to the butcher's, as they chatted over a comfortable cup of tea;

Catherine.

and the comment was not unwarranted. Her form was bent, her gray hair hung in a wild disheveled mass about her seamed and haggard countenance, and her wide blue eyes had a half-crazed look in them. "Hear how she mutters to herself," said the preacher's wife to her next-door neighbor, as the old woman passed by. "Who knows," returned the other, "but that the devil has taught her to charm evil sperits."

Had it been a century earlier, this harmless old woman would surely have been burned for a witch. She had an odd way, too, of disappearing now and then, for a week at a time, when suddenly the ox-cart would lumber into the village, and its aged occupant, more wretched and forlorn looking than ever, would hobble out at the door of the "hanted house," not to disappear again for mayhap a six month or more.

All this was extremely puzzling to the villagers, toward whom the old woman maintained the strictest secrecy as to her goings and comings, and had even refused to gratify their curiosity regarding her past history. However, notwithstanding the fact that no villager ever crossed her threshold, and that even the chil-

Catherine.

dren upon the streets taunted and tormented her, her wonderful knitting and sewing (and at half price, too) were not to be despised by the village merchants. She was known, too, at odd times, to take a turn in the harvest fields, and was reported by those employing her, to have given "a'most as much satisfaction as one of the reg'lar hands." What the old woman did with her earnings was beyond all mortal ken, for she stinted herself in the most parsimonious fashion.

Affairs went on at this rate for almost five years, when the village pastor (a man not unlike his people) accepted a new charge. His successor, an aged man of Southern birth (being in poor health), accepted the first vacant pastorate offering a change of climate. The heart of this big-souled Southerner was so full of love for God and man, that he seemed literally enveloped in a perpetual flood of sunshine; and who ever heard of sunshine that did not penetrate the darkest nook and cranny, and smile as beneficently upon the beggar in the gutter as upon my lord in his carriage?

The Rev. James Proctor Arnold was not slow in discovering the poor old woman, who for five

Catherine.

years had been the butt of the entire village. A glance at the pitiful face, with its great sorrowful eyes, which had in them the distressed look of some poor hunted animal, appealed to the good man's sympathy, and spoke more eloquently than words could have done, of the silent grief of a broken heart. His were the first feet that ever crossed her humble threshold, and slowly, and by degrees, his kindness won her confidence, and the poor old woman, so long estranged from all human sympathy, confided to him the pitiful tale of her life; a tale more sad by far than fiction's pen could ever paint. Sobbing bitterly, she pointed to a little time-worn crib (the same Tom Headly had fashioned for his unborn babe so long ago).

"'Tis all that's left me now," she moaned. Poor empty crib, and emptier hands. "I could not stay where they believed my poor good Tom done that awful deed," she sobbed, "and so I come here; here where no one knows him, or speaks his name. I work hard—oh, so hard, that I may see him at times, and take him some little gifts; but oh, he hardly knows me. He looks so wild, and shakes his head—his poor shaved head—the same I used to nestle in my bosom, and hush to sleep in yonder little crib. Oh, God! how hard—how hard it is to bear," and the poor heart-broken creature rocked herself to and fro in anguish which none but a mother, robbed by a more cruel hand than death, can ever feel.

CHAPTER VI.

<blockquote>
Who knows what earth needs, from earth's lowest creature,
No life can be pure in its purpose and strong in its strife,
And all life not be purer and stronger thereby.
—<i>Meredith.</i>
</blockquote>

ANOTHER August day had come, just such a sultry, rainy day as the memorable one five years before, when Tom Headly had been convicted of murder. And now, in the rude cabin she called her home, the patient hands of his poor old mother, the hands which had never before faltered in their ministry of labor and love, lay idle for the first time. The fever, which for ten days had racked the wasted form and filled the weary brain with weird fancies, was gone now, and over the wan old face there slowly crept the gray shadow of death. Beside her

Catherine.

sat the village pastor, and tenderly as might a woman have done, he wiped the dews of death from her forehead. Beseechingly the dying eyes fastened themselves upon his face, while the wasted toil-worn hand pointed feebly toward a rude wooden box. "The chest," she murmured faintly. Hastily the minister carried it to the bedside, and lifted the lid. Rolls of newly-made shirts and knitted socks were neatly folded therein, and beside them a little heap of money, the carefully saved earnings of the year. "For —T-Tom," she gasped, the words coming with an effort. "Tom shall have them, my good woman," answered the pastor comfortingly. "I will take them to him myself, and explain that they were the last gifts of his mother." Deeper settled the gray shadow upon the pallid face, and more difficult grew the breathing. "Come unto me, all ye that labor and are heavy laden, and I will give you rest." Softly and distinctly the man of God repeated the beautiful promise, but the dying woman heard it not. The poor mind was wandering again, and in fancy she cradled to her breast the babe of her youth. "The — cr-crib — I'll put you th-there — l-little

Catherine.

— Tom," she gasped. They were the last words she uttered; poor old Catherine was dead. The weary soul, which in life had known nothing but pain, had gone forth to that inheritance promised the faithful. "So He giveth his beloved sleep," softly repeated the minister, as he reverently closed the eyes of the dead.

> "Honest work for the day, honest hope for the morrow,
> Are these worth nothing more than the hand they make weary,
> The heart they have saddened, the life they leave dreary?
> Hush! the seven-fold heavens to the voice of the Spirit
> Echo: He that o'ercometh shall all things inherit."

THE EXPERIENCE OF A CORPSE

OR

THE FIRST NIGHT UNDERGROUND

* * *

THERE is not a city in America to which nature has been so prodigal of her gifts, as the beautiful "forest city of the South," Savannah, Ga. It was upon my first visit to Savannah that this story dates; and for the benefit of any disciple of Hamlin Garland who may scan its grewsome title, let me frankly state that it is not of the "new realistic" school, although its author (to coin a word from the new school) asserts its "veritism." Early in April, 1894, I was seated upon the veranda of the De Soto, listening to the music in Madison Square, and chatting with my old friend and college chum, Walter Calhoun, whom I had not

The Experience of a Corpse.

seen for five years. So sedulous had Calhoun been in praise of a beautiful South Carolinian (who, with her widowed mother, was to arrive upon the day following) that it was plain to be seen the shaft of the wily little god had been unerring in its aim. "Well, old boy," I exclaimed, "who would ever have thought to find you worshipping at the shrine of Eros. It is not worth while to dissemble! for it is plain that Cupid has marked you his victim." Calhoun lazily blew a wreath of smoke from beneath his tawny mustache, and tossing aside his cigar, replied: "It is not worth my while to dissemble, when I have especially invited you here to help me decide upon a difficulty that has tormented my brain for two years. Why there never was a schoolboy more foolishly in love than your humble servant Dr. Walter Calhoun, forty years of age, and a confirmed old bachelor." "What is the trouble, Walt?" I asked. "Does your divinity fail to reciprocate the tender passion?" "Upon the contrary," he replied, "I believe that she fancies me. Indeed, a score of fellows have urged me to go in and win, or forego the chase and give others a chance.

The Experience of a Corpse.

You see," he continued, dropping his voice to a confidential tone, "I fear the mother is a monomaniac, and yet you would never suspect it unless you knew her intimately, and perhaps not then. At times I fear my confounded profession has imbued me with a morbid terror of that accursed malady, and yet I can but believe the taint is there." "Perhaps much learning hath made thee mad," I returned, "and the fancied insanity is but a hallucination of thine own brain." "I would to God it were so," he replied with an energy that startled me. "The mother," he continued, "is reputed to be worth several million dollars; and while never giving a farthing to relieve poverty or carry on the Gospel, she is said to bequeath hundreds, nay thousands of dollars, to endow crematories." "Perhaps the old lady acts from a sanitary standpoint," I replied, "and prefers assisting her fellows in a line already too long neglected; for as a physician, you are of course aware that this is a subject agitating the minds of a great many scientists; and indeed, in my own opinion, it is but the feeble mutterings of a revolution,

The Experience of a Corpse.

which sooner or later must become the thunder of a demanding and fast increasing population." "Madame Courtney has a most eloquent defender," returned my friend, "and I admit that your argument is not without reason; but I have only acquainted you with a portion of her peculiarities upon this subject. Believe me, I would be the happiest man in Savannah, could I convince myself that she is not mad; for the experiences of my profession have been such that I can never bring myself to marry one whose blood is tainted with the awful heritage of insanity; and yet, for two years, I have permitted myself to linger under the spell of the charms of this woman's daughter, hoping against hope that I may find myself mistaken." "Well, well, old fellow, cheer up," I replied, "for I doubt not but that the professional experiences of which you speak have rendered you morbid upon this subject, and that after all, things are not half so bad as you picture them." "At any rate," returned my friend arising, "I will not burden you with any more of my troubles to-night, and to-morrow you shall have an opportunity of judging for yourself," and warmly wringing my hand, we bade each other goodnight.

I admit that it was with great curiosity that I looked forward to meeting Madame Courtney and her daughter Catherine, and it was not until the following evening that Calhoun presented them to me. The mother, although rather petite, gave one the impression of being somewhat stately; for having been born and reared in Charleston, S. C., she had that dignified bearing, and queenly old-time grace, which seems the heritage of the Charlestonian. The daughter — Ah! how can I describe her? She was only a fair-faced, golden-haired girl. I had seen many faces by far more fair, but she had a magnetism, a certain naïveté that set her apart; a strongly marked individuality that claimed your attention when fairer faces than hers were near. Perhaps the most striking feature of her countenance was her eyes, now blue as the azure of a summer sky, again grey and flashing, and anon — a pale beryl, like a sudden glimpse of old ocean, when foam-tossed it dimples in the sunshine. These wonderful

The Experience of a Corpse.

changeable eyes looked out from under a pair of straight dark brows. These formed a pretty contrast to the mass of golden ringlets which curled about the broad low brow. Upon first beholding these two faces, I was curiously impressed with a sense of their familiarity, although quite positive I had never seen either of them before. It was as if two portraits with which I had been familiar from childhood had suddenly come to life, and stepped from their frames. I did not reveal my impression to Calhoun, but I felt sure it was shared by the fair Catherine, whom I frequently observed gazing at me in a perplexed sort of way, as though fain to solve the mystery which puzzled my own brain. That night my dreams were troubled; I was vainly laboring to place Madame Courtney and pretty Catherine. A month later, having been thrown daily into the society of the two, I would have sworn that Calhoun's impression of Madame Courtney was an absurd delusion. Never by word or act, had she betrayed the slightest symptom of hallucination. On the contrary, she was all that a brilliant, cultured, fascinating woman can be; while I—heaven pity me—was

The Experience of a Corpse.

so madly, so passionately in love with her daughter, that knowing every prolonged moment of bliss spent at her side but added to the hopeless misery of a love my honor forbade me reveal, still lingered. In vain I pleaded with Calhoun to offer his love to Catherine, endeavoring to make him feel with me the ridiculousness of his opinion of Madame Courtney.

Finally he came to me one morning and said: "I have arranged for a drive to-night, and if you will make one of the party I will prove the truth of my assertion regarding Madame Courtney's mania. I have but one request to make: assist me in so closely engrossing the ladies in conversation that they will fail to observe our entrance to Bonaventure cemetery; and once there, note its impression upon Madame Courtney." Always willing to please Calhoun, and anxious to draw affairs to a climax, I consented. It was a perfect evening for a drive, and as we whirled down the broad avenues, magnificent in their rich, flowery, tropical foliage, there was wafted on the balmy, languorous, flower-scented air the merry voices of children at play, mingled with the clatter of

The Experience of a Corpse.

passing vehicles, and the peculiar cries of an occasional negro fruit or vegetable vender. The beautiful face opposite my own shone fairer than the silvery stars in the azure firmament, and not unlike those stars, methought, forever beyond my reach. My love for this girl, in its intensity and utter hopelessness, had become an agony well-nigh unbearable, and it was with difficulty that I assisted in engaging the ladies in conversation, while the carriage rolled noiselessly through the gates of the grand old cemetery. The last crimson rays of departing day seemed suddenly to have merged into the purple shadows of twilight. We were shut in by a magnificent archway, a grand old Gothic cathedral not made by hands, the architecture of nature. Gigantic oaks which have withstood the storms of more than a century, reaching out their giant limbs, form this mighty archway; and gleaming like silver sheen among the dark green leaves, depends such heavy growth of old gray Spanish moss, as to give the spot a weird, almost supernatural, appearance. It is as if nature, in bedecking this hallway of her dead, had placed thereon the seal

The Experience of a Corpse.

of solemnity. The sudden merging of day into twilight attracted the attention of the ladies, who glanced up in awe at the solemn beauty of the scene. Suddenly a tombstone gleamed white in the distance. A wild cry of terror rent the air. "My God — I am in a cemetery," shrieked Madame Courtney, and fell fainting in her daughter's arms. "How dare you thus disregard my mother's feelings, knowing her aversion to a cemetery, Dr. Calhoun," asked the daughter sternly. Calhoun, muttering an apology, gave an order to the driver, who turning the horses about, drove rapidly to Thunderbolt Inn, where no time was lost in procuring restoratives. How like a corpse the aged woman looked, as in the fading twilight she lay pillowed within the tender arms which refused to be released of their burden. Suddenly, with a deep shuddering groan the prostrate woman opened her eyes and sat up. Although shaking as if from an ague fit, she seemed possessed of a dormant energy. With flashing eyes she turned toward Calhoun, and haughtily exclaimed: "Through your utter disregard of my feelings, in thus exposing me to suffering you know to be inevitable, you have, sir, forever forfeited my friendship." Calhoun feebly endeavored to remonstrate, but she ignored him, and addressed herself to me. "You have known me at least long enough, Mr. De Saussure, to know that I am neither erratic or superstitious," she said, "and after this painful scene, I feel that an explanation is due from me." "Spare yourself, my dear madame, at least until some future time when you are stronger," I replied. "No — I must speak now, when I feel most deeply," she answered imperiously. It was a strange, never-to-be-forgotten scene. The fair girl, silent, and with a scared expression upon her lovely countenance; the mother, trembling, imperious, and with the air of a tragedy queen; these two sat facing us. Calhoun, white and wretched, gazed beseechingly at the girl, while I waited with impatient curiosity the result of this evening so tragic in its beginning and necessarily so momentous in its results.

"As you know," began the old lady, "I am a Buddhist; and our religion, so ancient, so beautiful, so long despised by the people of this nation, is at last finding favor with some of its

The Experience of a Corpse.

deepest thinkers. You are doubtless aware of our belief in rebirth and constant transmigration of soul until the blissful perfection of Nirvana is attained. My experience, which I am about to relate, and which altered my entire future," she continued, "dates back some centuries ago, when I, the daughter of Christian parents, lived upon this earth, died, and was given the usual Christian burial. Perhaps a vainer, more self-worshipful creature than was I, never existed (for I was absolutely beautiful), and my retribution was such as the direst torture of a Christian hell has failed to portray. It was — THE EXPERIENCE OF A CORPSE, OR THE FIRST NIGHT UNDERGROUND. Oh, ye saints of Buddha! the experience of *that first night underground!* The spirit which had worshipped at no shrine save that of its own beautiful body, was compelled (for a short space after death) to retain its tenement of clay. Ah! ye gods, the very remembrance of that night is enough to drive one mad. Deep coffined in the cold sepulchral ground, far from all the sweet familiar sights and sounds of nature! Never to see the sun arise in his majestic splendor, never to

The Experience of a Corpse.

hear the birds sing, or to smell the freshness of the morning air! Never to watch the moon drift in her silver radiance among the clouds; or the stars sparkle like jewels in the vaulted heavens! To be compelled to lie in that loathsome bed and realize the face I worshipped undergo all the hideous changes so soon to rob it of its divine beauty! To watch the sinking of the features; the horror of decay with its deadly work of worms, and at the end, the hideous, grinning, socketless skull! But why torture you with the repetition of an experience the ghastliness of which baffles human skill to portray? One night to me was as a hundred years, and this experience of centuries ago lingers in my mind with more intensity than do the occurrences of yesterday.

When released from the hell of my imprisonment, I sacredly vowed that my life should be more humble, and that I would spare no pains in establishing the only true mode of burial; and while faithful to my trust, spending my fortune freely to this end, I have ever been slow in repeating the experience which led thereto, knowing that the cold, incredulous world

The Experience of a Corpse.

would but scoff at me." Suddenly — as one awakening from a dream I reached forward, and seizing the old lady's hands exclaimed: "Dear Madame Courtney, something stirs my soul as in a dim, vague fancy. I seem to have heard this tale centuries ago in some other life. I am playing upon the beach with a little girl whose face is very like Catherine's, her name — is — Coy." The old lady started violently. "Nirvana of the saints made perfect," she exclaimed, "it is Catherine's middle name; it was the name of my father; go on! go on!" "We reached the years of maturity," I continued, "and I loved Coy, as I never loved anything else on earth. We were to have been married, when something intervened which prevented it; but it is all as a dream to me. A dream from which I seem to have awakened before it was finished." "Pennoyer," — it was Catherine who spoke, and she called me by my mother's name. Softer than the zephyrs, sweeter than the magnolia blooms which they kissed, was her voice, while her face shone with the tranfiguration of a passionate, idolatrous love. "Then you have not forgotten

The Experience of a Corpse.

your Coy — you love me still." There seemed nothing unmaidenly in the girl's advance; on the contrary, she was the embodiment of modesty, and simple naïveté. "Surely Pennoyer—" she went on, "you remember our last evening together upon the beach? How soon I should have become your wife, had not my jealous and cowardly cousin taken your life. Ah me! how in my anguish I longed for death." She was kneeling at my feet now, clasping both of my hands in her own little fair ones. How vividly from the dull rust of bygone years, came back the memory of my last evening with this girl whom I had worshipped so madly — who was to have been my wife — and yet whose very name I had forgotten until the present moment. Was it all a dream? No — my hands clasped firmly the little fingers placed so confidingly within them. I forgot the presence of others, and lived but in the past, as I clasped to my heart once more, the beautiful creature who knelt at my feet — covering her face, her lips, her brow, with passionate kisses.

I was aroused from my happy forgetfulness

The Experience of a Corpse.

by the shrill voice of Calhoun calling the driver to stop. I had forgotten his presence, and glanced at him now for the first time. His face was set and livid, like that of a corpse. "Stop, driver," he shrieked wildly, "that I may rid myself of these cursed lunatics while I am still sane;" and dashing himself from the vehicle, he disappeared. The evening paper of the following day chronicled the sudden departure of Dr. Walter Calhoun for New York, from whence he would sail for Europe to remain indefinitely; and as the engagement of his friend to the beautiful South Carolinian was announced soon after, it was pretty generally believed by Madame Grundy and her host of followers that the engagement had much to do with the Doctor's sudden departure. There are few in this materialistic age who will give credence to this tale, as happy in its sequel as it is grewsome in title. It would be difficult to find a happier couple than myself and wife; while my mother-in-law (whose aid-de-camp I am in abetting all her efforts toward reform in burial) pronounces me "the best fellow in the world." Should you, my reader, chance in the near future to

The Experience of a Corpse.

find yourself in the proud old city of Charleston, S. C., and while strolling along its battery behold the erection of a palatial mansion, you will please to remember it is the future residence of Mr. and Mrs. George Pennoyer De Saussure, and their loved mother, whose gift it is to her children. For the benefit of the incredulous, I will add that Dr. P.—, one of Savannah's most prominent physicians, and brave soldiers who wore the gray, will bear me out as to the idiosyncrasies of Madame Courtney, whom he has often heard relate her "experience of a corpse, or the first night underground."

LOVE'S FIRST CONQUEST

LEGGENDARIO

* * *

IN the prehistoric ages, before the world was peopled, and Eros, child of Heaven and Earth dwelt here alone, Spring and Autumn had never had a birth. In the southern land of sunshine and blue skies perpetual Summer reigned, while in the far-off north grim Winter forever held his sway.

In a spot on the banks of the Nile, where in the early morn lotus blossoms opened their blue eyes to greet the sun, which in majestic splendor blazed in the heavens like a globe of fire; and where the feathery palm-tree, airy acacia, and fragrant mimosa grow in all their luxuriousness, entwined in vines which trail in wild profusion, until their varied and gorgeous blossoms float in brilliant colors upon the crimson

Love's First Conquest.

tinted waters of the Nile, in this spot of brightness, warmth, and tropical luxury, dwelt young Eros, child of Love.

This had been the trysting place of Heaven and Earth, and the birthplace of their child. He reveled in the beauty about him, for while from one parent he inherited purity and æstheticism, from the other he partook of the deepest capability for sensuous enjoyment; and these elements, seemingly at variance, were the necessary constituents to a perfect nature.

Hither and thither wandered the lad at his own sweet will. Gorgeous-hued birds flocked to his call, and ferocious beasts of the desert fawned at his feet with the docility of the lamb, for the mysticism of Heaven was his.

At times the young god tired of the sights and sounds, the beasts and birds about him, and longed for conquest and more extended fields; for within his soul slept the embryo germ, which in future years was to make him conqueror of the world.

Could he have realized the extended realm, that in after years evolution should assign him; could he have beheld the entire earth peopled,

Love's First Conquest.

and himself crowned conqueror of them all, more patiently would his soul have possessed itself; but though immortal, he knew nothing of his destiny, and his heart panted with the inborn desire of a conqueror.

One afternoon, when the African sun burned fiercely in the Heavens, and not a breeze stirred the palm-trees above his head, young Eros indulged in fanciful dreams of the far-off land of ice and snow.

"Naught could be more beautiful," he murmured, "than this sensuous spot of warmth and fragrance which gave me birth, and yet my soul pineth for a glimpse of the far-off mountains of the north, for a breath from its cool pine forests; yet — how dare I venture to that spot where perpetual Winter reigns." Long he pondered in silence, when suddenly, with a glad cry he sprang to his feet. The fertility of his imagination had given birth to a sudden inspiration, which filled his soul with wild joy. He laughed aloud, as hastily he entwined his bow and arrow in a brilliant mass of flowers. Great wreaths of the same festooned his body, and adorned his neck and brow. As he moved

Love's First Conquest.

swiftly forward, the sun gleaming blood-bright among the floating gold of his tresses, and glancing among the scarlet and purple of the brilliant flowers which adorned him, he made a fitting picture for the rich coloring and gorgeous tropical beauty about him. Swift as the wind moved the god, his fair body and burnished tresses absorbing, as he went, the fierce intensity of the African sun.

"Burn fierce, and fiercer still," he cried. "Thou sun which blazeth like a globe of fire in heaven's clear blue, send down thy fiery shafts until they pierce my soul, permeate my being, and make me thy very child; for to-day go I forth upon my first mission. Without thee I fail, by thy aid I stand the proud conqueror of a mighty achievement; for I seek, O Sun! to melt the heart of the cold, unapproachable North, that mine own fair clime, and thine, may find favor in his sight. I seek by device, known alone to Love, and by the soft, sweet amorous wooing of our own fair land, to kiss to life the hidden passion of his frozen heart, until in fond desire he clasp the Southland close, and print upon her burning lips a nuptial kiss."

Love's First Conquest.

Thus spoke Eros, child of Love. And the Sun replied:—

"Lo! thou child of Heaven and Earth, behold, thou shalt reign forever, and all things above and beneath shall be subject to thee. Speed on, bear in thine arms and upon thy bosom the sensuous warmth and fragrance of our own fair land of sunshine and blue skies; and fear thou not, for in the land of eternal winter, where never a flower bloomed, they shall not depart from thee, for they are thine heritage."

Once more the young god laughed aloud, while onward, with the velocity of the wind, he sped, never wearying, until, lo! a dazzling thing of fragrance, warmth, and beauty, he paused upon the threshold of the land of eternal snow. Mightier than the coming of a host of armed kings were the silent footsteps of the god of love, as burning with the warmth of his tropical sunland, his rosy feet rested upon the snow-clad mountains of the far-away north. A tall pine tree shook its fringe of feathery snow upon his sunny head, and the fierce blast of winter whistled about his unprotected form, but this child of fire and flame heeded them not.

Love's First Conquest.

"I come, O North!" he cried, "in the name of the fair Sunland of perpetual summer. See, I have borne her to thee within mine arms, and upon my bosom." But the cold North opened not his frozen lips.

"See, O Northland! is she not beautiful?" cried Eros, as for an instant the sunland gleamed athwart his vision. Shyly the flower-like face of Summer smiled into the cold face of Winter, as softly she approached him, shedding with every step a shower of sensuous fragrance. Upon his regal head she placed a wreath of blossoms, and soft, her fair young fingers touched his brow, and warm, her fragrant breath caressed his cheek. Strange thrills ran through his gigantic being; a warmth he ne'er had felt before penetrated his veins and caused the mighty heart to throb, which naught had ever agitated. The warm magnetic touch exhilarated him, the fair, luminous presence intoxicated him, while to her the inflexible impenetrability of his majestic bearing pleased and overawed her. Each stood, magnetized, gazing upon the other in speechless rapture. Only an instant did the flower-soft touch of Summer lin-

Love's First Conquest.

ger upon the brow of Winter; only an instant did her fragrant breath float across his cheek. Fair Summer knew her power, coquettishly she turned away — when, lo! his hauteur vanished like the mist before the sun, and stretching forth his mighty arms, closely he circled her fair form, crying in voice as deep as distant thunder: —

"Come to me, O thou beauteous bride of the fair land of summer." And in that close embrace the Earth reeled and trembled, and as their lips met in one long nuptial kiss the fields of snow melted from the earth like a river and were absorbed by the luminous presence of Summer, whose fair hands strewed flowers in their stead.

Two flower-tipped arrows had sped from the unerring hand of the designing Eros, accomplishing their purpose; and peeping from behind a clump of pines, his sunny locks gemmed with their melting snow, he laughed aloud in joyfulness, and with the proud tread of a conqueror, sped back on swift wings to his sunny nook on the banks of the River Nile, there to laugh and dream of how, through him, fair Summer had conquered and slain proud Winter.

Love's First Conquest.

Forgotten were the beasts and birds, which in bygone days had charmed his careless hours, and for one whole long year the little god sat still and smiled, and dreamed about the mysteries of life and love. And then — once more he hied him to the spot where fair queen Summer had conquered her lord.

When, lo! there awaited him a mystery by far more great; for up into his face there smiled two lovely twins, the offspring of the mystic union of the seasons. Young Spring — so like her mother in all tender loveliness, and sturdy Autumn, softened type of his stern father.

Hence, in the prehistoric ages, Love first established, through birth of those fair babes, that law which men still seek to understand, the philosophy of "the survival of the fittest."

A CONFEDERATE FOR A DAY

• • •

It is possible that the older residents of the historical "Hill City," Lynchburg, Va., will recognize in the hero of this little tale one of her prominent business men; and among the splendid galaxy who wore the gray and whose proud names and heroic deeds will descend in historic glory to unborn nations, none were more brave than Lynchburg's "Confederate for a day." He was such a tiny tot, blue eyed and golden haired, but no heart throbbed with greater loyalty to the Southern cause than that of this little embryo soldier. Longings to join the splendid company which marched so proudly from the Hill City under General Jubal Early's command filled the breast of the little lad, but alas!—he was *only ten years old*, and such a *little* lad at that. Visions of how *strategy* might

A Confederate for a Day.

prevail filled his small brain; and when brothers followed father in the proudest, bravest army that ever graced the globe, his resentment of the *barrier of youth* knew no limit. By continual imploring he had prevailed upon his brothers to make him a cannon large enough to carry a minie ball, and he became very dexterous in the use of it. There is perhaps no life, consumed by any earnest desire, that the longing is not in some sense gratified, and the gala-day of this boy's life came to him when Jubal Early marshalled his forces and beat back Hunter's army in their attempt to take Lynchburg. Little dreamed the fond mother, as she prayed at home while the distant din of battle sent terror to her heart, that in the rear of that army, marching with the boys in gray, triumphant of heart, and carrying his little cannon in hand, was her golden-haired baby. All day long was heard the ceaseless boom of cannon and the hail of shells was continuous — but the boy felt no alarm. Proudly he fired his cannon with the rest, and as the smoke poured forth, and the sound added to the tumult which led to Hunter's retreat, his heart beat high with hope that he

A Confederate for a Day.

might at least have lessened the Yankee force by one. But the heart of childhood, after all, how full of love and forgiveness it is (as the sequel of this tale will prove), and how beautiful an example of the Master's words: "Unless ye become as one of these." The day drew to a close, and Hunter had retired, leaving victory to the boys in gray, and they, slowly, and worn with excitement, marched back to the city. The little soldier's brother, splendid in his uniform of gray, and proud in the glory of his sixteen years, was among the soldiers stationed that day at Morman's Fort; and when, upon reaching Halsey's farm that evening, he found little Edward awaiting him, his golden curls matted, his little face begrimed with powder, great was his surprise. "I say, Jimmie," said the child, as the soldiers marched away, "let us go back over the field and hunt things." Jimmie was but a child, too; it was only since he had donned the gray that he "put off childish things," and he replied: "All right, Ed, run on and I'll sit here and wait for you; but mind, you musn't be gone long."

The child sauntered on, picking up here and

A Confederate for a Day.

there grim reminders of the day's carnage, when suddenly he espied a trophy he had not counted upon. A gleam of hated blue greeted his eyes from beneath a clump of bushes; a real, live Yankee. "Gemany!" muttered the lad, "if only Jimmie had come along we might have captured him." "Hey! boy!" called the soldier. Some of the courage he had felt when the cannons were roaring and the gray uniforms thick about, suddenly deserted him. He was all alone now, and face to face with a Yankee soldier. "Don't be scared," called the soldier, "I ain't going to hurt you; I just want to know if there are any more rebel soldiers around." Thoughts of diplomacy in so small a bosom never entered the blue coat's mind. Suddenly the boy's courage returned with redoubled force. Visions of taking this Yank by strategy filled the bosom of the little "Johnny." "I should say so!" he replied. "The woods are just *full* of them, and Jubal Early's army just below you yonder. You're not the *first* one they have shot spying on our ground." "All right," replied the soldier. "Go bring your men and tell them I *surrender*."

A Confederate for a Day.

Off ran "the Confederate of a day." It was the one supreme moment of his life. He was breathless. His words came by starts. "Brother!" he exclaimed, "I've caught one. A scared live Yankee. He thinks these woods are full of us. He's surrendered—he wants to be took." When did the fear of danger ever present itself to Southern heart? "Oh! is *that* all he wants," replied the young soldier, proudly straightening himself to his full height. "Well, I'll *take* him all right." Just then a young lieutenant came up, and together the three went forward, and took charge of the surrendered soldier. "He's *my man*," said little Ed as he proudly led the way; "you all only have a *hand* in this, 'cause you got on *uniform*." "All right, Eddie," laughed the young lieutenant. "We will give you all the *glory*, and we will take the *spoils*." The soldier in question was but a lad, too; a mere boy of eighteen; he disarmed the boy in blue. A few hundred feet from the prisoner was hitched his magnificent bay. "I'll take charge of the horse," said the lieutenant; and carrying the Yankee's arms, he rode proudly away, while the boy in

A Confederate for a Day.

blue, weary and downcast, marched slowly between the two brothers to Lynchburg. Little Edward began to feel sorry for the prisoner now that he had lost his liberty, and the beautiful holiness of childhood asserted itself, and was, after all, but an illustration of the fact (made prominent by General John B. Gordon in his eloquent lecture upon 'The Last Days of the Confederacy'), that never in the annals of history had such an interchange of kindness existed as that shown between the North and South in the late Civil War.

"Aint you all hungry?" asked the child. "Yes," replied the prisoner, "I have had *nothing* to eat for twenty-four hours." "Never mind," answered the boy, "when I see whereabouts they *put* you, I'll carry you something to eat. Where are you all from?" "From Philadelphia," was the reply. "Oh!" cried the child, "You know my uncle, and my Cousin Jimmie?" "Philadelphia is a big place, lad," answered the soldier. "Well, they live in that part you call *Bridesburg!*" said the boy. "Oh, I know every one there; *that* is my home," answered the soldier. "What are their names?" The boy

A Confederate for a Day.

gave them. "Why, Jimmie is my *best* friend," he replied. More and more downcast grew "the Confederate of a day." Closely he followed the boy in blue, waiting until he found him imprisoned in the office of the Provost Marshal (the room now over Gregory's bookstore), and then hastening to his anxious mother he poured into her astonished ears his adventures of the day. He had captured Cousin Jimmie's friend — the friend was starving — and he had promised him food. What Southern mother, think you, ever refused a hungry soldier food, though his garments were blue instead of gray? A smoking hoe-cake, between the buttered slices of which rested generous slices of ham, was soon in the hands of the eager little lad, who sped quickly toward the office of the Provost Marshal, where further difficulties awaited him, the guard positively refusing to permit him to pass. "But I *will* pass," he exclaimed. "I done took that Yankee prisoner, and I promised to tote him something to eat, and I'm going to give it to him myself, too." "You can't pass," said the guard, "if you give me the food I'll see that he gets

A Confederate for a Day.

it." "I'll not give it to you," answered the boy stoutly. "I know — you all want to eat it yourselves." One of the lad's brothers was a telegraph messenger boy, and often passed the guards with messages. So, nothing daunted, the determined boy hastened to Major Gault, then in command, where permission to pass was instantly granted him. The guard displayed his white teeth in a broad smile as he passed the lad, and exclaimed: "You'll get thar boy. You'd bribe Peter for the key, if you couldn't get into glory." "I got a *sure* passport there —" said the boy brightly. "I won't have to do any red-tape business." A moment later the grateful food was placed in the hands of the half-famished soldier, and hastening to a near spring, the child procured him a bucket of water. A few days later the soldier was exchanged. Years have come and gone since then, and faithfully, but in vain, sought "the Confederate of a day," for that Bridesburg boy in blue. Among the mighty phalanx of unknown dead, he sleeps in Southern soil, unmindful that his ashes mingle with that of those who wore the gray. And not until our

A Confederate for a Day.

"Confederate of a day" hears the command from the Great General of the universe to "Come up higher," shall he meet and greet the soldier boy in blue, where blue and gray blend in harmony as fair as in the clouds which sweep the heavens.

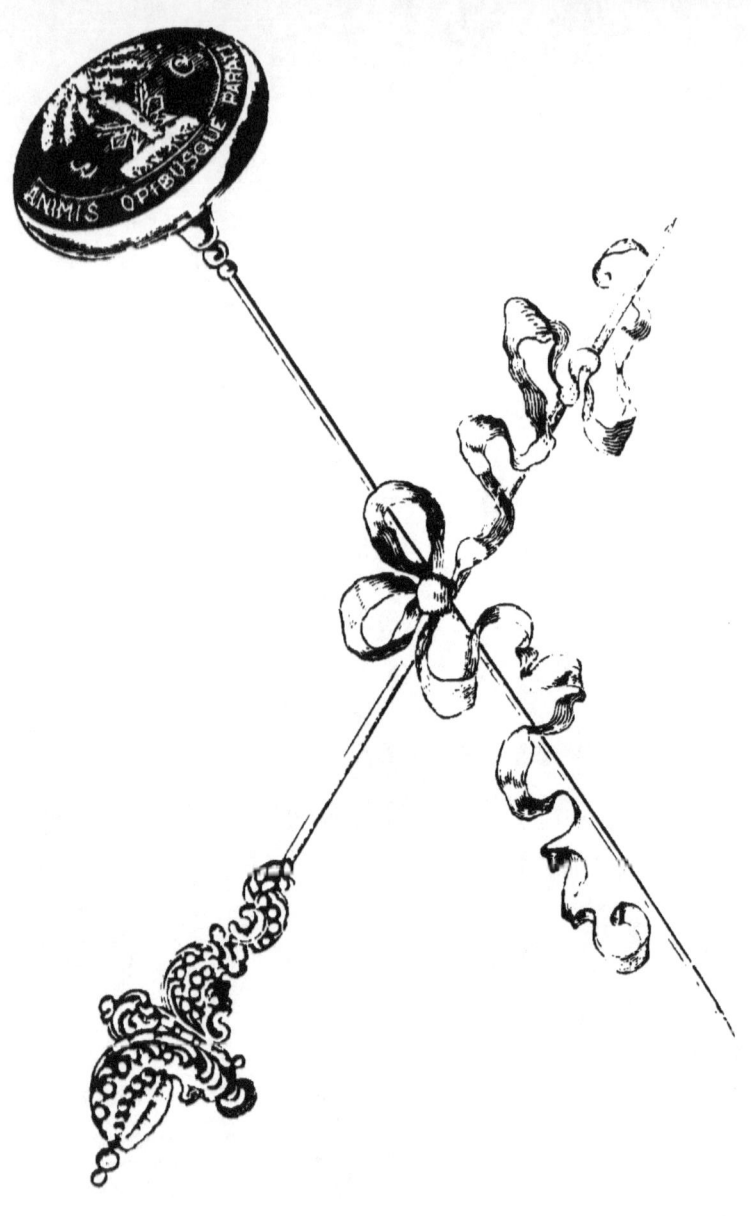

THE TWO HAT PINS
∙ ∙ ∙

IN the daintiest of a dainty boudoir in a palatial home in Louisville, Kentucky (city of beautiful women), within a Dresden jewel-case lay two hat pins, still warm from contact with the golden-brown head against which they so recently nestled. One was a jeweled thing of beauty, an amethyst of unusual size, purity, and warmth, surrounded by diamonds; the other, a Confederate button, bearing the South Carolina coat of arms, and the familiar motto, "Parati animis opibusque."

"You are a pretty thing," exclaimed the jeweled pin to the button, "to be placed upon so familiar a footing with me; and I wish you to know in the beginning, there can be no intimacy between us; for although your companionship be forced upon me, I shall ignore you. I am a Tiffany pin of the purest water, while

The Two Hat Pins.

you are merely a gold-washed brass button, which none but a dowdy Southern girl would dream of associating with *me*."

"I cannot boast of wealth or precious stones," replied the button, "but true to the land of my birth, I am proud of the record which money cannot buy, and which was won through valor and bloodshed. I graced the sleeve of as brave an arm as ever carried Southern flag, and for four long weary years faithfully we bore the Florida flag (barring the time we languished in Northern prison); and now, right proud am I to grace the head of one who prizes me for what I am worth."

The conversation was interrupted by the entrance of the owner of the pin, accompanied by a girl friend, who, bending over the case, eagerly grasped the button, and studied it carefully.

"Mary!" she exclaimed, "You always were the luckiest girl in creation in the realization of all your desires. Why, I have asked every soldier in Louisville for a real Confederate button, and while each has promised me one, all their promises remain unfulfilled."

The Two Hat Pins.

"Did you ever see a Kentucky man who would refuse a woman his head, if she asked it," answered the proud owner of the button, "but to give it to her, that is a different matter."

"I would give anything for such a hat pin," went on the friend. "Did you say it was a South Carolina or a Florida man who gave it to you, Mary?"

"Both," laughed the girl; "Captain Smith is a South Carolinian by birth, and a Floridian by adoption, and as gloriously big-hearted, dignified, and elegant as South Carolinians always are. To be sure," she added, "all Southern men are generous, but a South Carolina or Virginia gentleman has just a *little something* in mannerism which I miss in men from other States. For where in the United States could you find another so princely and courteous in bearing as General M. C. Butler of South Carolina, or Generals Fitzhugh and Custis Lee of Virginia. Very princes among men are these; gentlemen of the old régime, which are born, and not bred so. They make one long for the old South, and that which in the rush and

The Two Hat Pins.

hurry of to-day is fast becoming extinct; that rare elegance, grace, and magnificence of bearing which stamp a man's superiority before he speaks."

"So far as that goes," answered Bernice, "Kentucky men are good enough for me. Even you must concede the fact, Mary, that *our* men (leaving the women out of the question) are the handsomest in America; and I love them for being unable to refuse a woman anything, even if they never intend giving it to her." The two girls laughed merrily.

"This is pretty," exclaimed Mary, handing her friend the jeweled pin.

"Yes, beautiful," she replied, "but any one can have such a pin who has the money to buy it. I am sure you prize the Confederate pin most."

"I would, save for the fact that Clive gave me this," she replied, tenderly replacing the jeweled pin. "I always prize most what Clive gives me, and he gives more beautiful things to me than I desire him to do, because you know, Bernice, we are not to be rich. Ours will be but a modest little home."

The Two Hat Pins.

"Yes, Mary, you are a mystery to me," rattled Bernice. "The idea of discarding Tom Nash, with his *princely fortune*, for a poor young fellow like Clive, struggling for a livelihood."

"But I love Clive," answered Mary simply, "and, like the Confederate button, money cannot buy that."

"And such a changed girl as you are, too," went on her friend. "Why I told Robert Staunton (whom you had never met) that you were the biggest flirt in Kentucky, and he told me afterwards that for an hour he thought your absent-mindedness but assumed coquettishness, until he discovered you were so much in love with some one that you could not even show a passing interest in another; and that he had, in consequence, a poor opinion of my judgment of a flirt. But you *were* the biggest flirt in Kentucky before you met Clive, you know you were, Mary."

"Yes, and all my past life seems so empty. Everything seems to me to date back to the hour I first met and loved Clive. Our home, though ever so humble, shall be a paradise, because perfect love for each other and God

The Two Hat Pins.

reigns in our hearts. Oh! Bernice, I do so wish every girl I meet could be as royally happy as I am."

"Mary, you are a dear little goose," answered Bernice." "And I reckon you are right in painting a halo about your Clive's head, for I have never seen a woman change as his love has changed you. Why, the Mary I knew, would have flirted with Bob Staunton until she would have blinded him to every other girl in our set, until she saw fit to discard him."

"You should be pleased then, Bernice, with the change," smiled Mary, "for I notice that Mr. Staunton is not too blind to admire you prodigiously."

"Where shall you live when you are married?" asked Bernice.

"In Richmond, Virginia, the beautiful, dreamy old Confederate Capital," answered Mary, "and you shall visit me, Bernice, and I know some charming soldiers there, who will give you a whole uniform of buttons, if you will accept themselves as well, for they asked me to find them a Kentucky sweetheart."

"Bravo," laughed Bernice. "They will find

The Two Hat Pins.

the Kentucky girls not behind Virginia girls in 'discarding' them, too, when tired of them."

The two girls laughed, and arm in arm sauntered from the room.

The hat pins gazed at each other. The jeweled pin broke the silence.

"I am sorry I was so hasty in my opinion of you," she exclaimed. "I see you are in better repute than I dreamed one in so cheap a garb could be, and I am glad to know it, as we are so intimately associated."

"I trust," answered the Confederate button, that the conversation of the two girls may have impressed you with the fact that there are some things which money cannot buy; and that there is a truth, grand beyond conception, in the teachings of Paul, wherein he says:—

"In lowliness of mind, let each esteem others better than themselves."

A CHAPTER FROM A BOY'S LIFE

* * *

THE hero of this simple tale is not a lad too tender for any boyish sport. It is only in his heart-life and beauty of soul that he stands alone. Like a lovely bud, growing daily more beauteous as it attains perfect fruition, so the baby, as it developed into boyhood, and the boy as he is developing into manhood, grows more exquisite, in complete oneness with God. He was a queer, original baby, whom his mother said came into her life because she had "asked God for him," and whom she said she named and dedicated to God before his birth. A baby with features as beautifully molded as a girl's, and coloring as exquisite as the petal of a rose. The child's worship for his mother, and hers for him, was something the angels must have smiled upon. Very often he would sit at her feet, and give voice to whatever was in her mind, so exactly seemed their natures in accord with each other. The child seemed a living demonstration of the broad, beautiful philosophy of Emerson, which his mother loved so well. His little soul overflowed with beauty, truth, and holiness, of which he was a revelation in the highest degree, yet withal, full of the pranks of childhood. One summer morning, his curls tossed in golden fleece about his shoulders, his dainty white gown bespattered with mud, the little fellow laboriously, and with sturdy, determined little fists, threw up shovelful after shovelful of mud. A man in passing by paused to look at the pretty picture, and called out: "What you trying to do, boy! dig a well?" The child paused, and with serious gravity replied: "No—I'm digging for the devil." "For the what?" said the man; "for the devil," answered the child. The man laughed until he wiped the tears from his cheeks, and replied: "Why, you'd run like a good fellow if you found him, boy! They say he has horns!" "*I* wouldn't be scared," answered the baby contemptuously, "*I am God's child*, and nothing can hurt me. Mamma says there *is no devil*, only the naughty in people's hearts. Tom Jones says 'there just is,' and that he 'lives under the ground,' but I've digged three days and he hasn't come up yet." "You better give him up as a bad job," answered the man. A gorgeously hued butterfly flitted by, and dropping his shovel the child was off like a flash to give it chase. It was the habit of this baby to daily bedeck his mother's writing desk with violets and roses, which it was his great pleasure to gather for her. "They are God's pretty little thoughts," said the child, "and as you write and look at them, mamma, you'll think of God and me."

One day he met a baby at his gate, a baby as dirty and forlorn as he was spotless and beautiful. "Why do you not wash?" said the child. "God must feel sorry to see you so dirty. The little birds wash, and God washes all the trees and flowers with rain and dew. When I get *big*, I'll give soap, and brooms, and vaseline to everyone like you. You could put the vaseline on your face to make it well. Here —take this rose, and when you see how sweet and clean it is, you, too, will wash." Later— when the baby was a baby no longer, but wore

A Chapter from a Boy's Life.

trousers and jackets, a playmate remarked to him: "How could you keep from hitting Tom Brown when he tore your kite up?" The boy plucked a rose from the bush and threw it to the ground. "See how *still* the bush is," he replied; "it just blooms on — as sweet as ever — and the sun shines — and everything in nature is always so still — and grand, no matter how agitated people are, that it always seems to me — a great teacher — that *speaks* to us from God — to be always calm — and still — and smiling; and then when I am angry, I try to be still and say to myself — I am God's child — His life — and love — are within me — I must not mar His temple with anger. I believe Tom Brown will be hurt by that act, because no one can do another an unkindness without hurting himself." "Where do you learn to think so many things?" asked the little friend. "I will tell you," answered the boy. "Mamma and myself 'wait before the Lord' every day." "Do you mean pray?" asked the other. "No," was the reply. "Of course I pray, but not when I wait. We wait silently before God — while He flows into us His spirit, peace, and all

A Chapter from a Boy's Life.

health and joy. Our souls and our bodies receive the quiet, certain blessing. Why, I never go away from home that I do not wish for my dear little pine pillow I brought from Pass Christian, Mississippi, and which has such sweet associations, because I have put my head upon it and 'waited' so many times before God for His blessing." "What do you hear when you wait?" asked the child. "Nothing," answered the boy; "I only realize God's presence — and *practice* His presence just as mamma practices on the piano." "That's queer," said the child. "I never heard of such things." "Yes — it is queer," was the reply, "but, oh, it just helps you *every way*. I would sooner go without dinner than without the waiting. It keeps all harm and trouble from you, even sickness; but if pain does come — it is only God's lesson to us to teach us patience and draw us closer to Him. We cannot get so near God in *any other way*, as we can in this waiting in silence before Him. You know one of the promises is — 'He that dwelleth in the secret place of the Most High shall abide under the shadow of the Almighty.'"

A Chapter from a Boy's Life.

One evening the boy sat beside his mother, literally drinking in the melody of one of Beethoven's sonatas; suddenly he interrupted her. "Mamma," he said, "I feel as though I could follow that melody if I had a flute." The mother arose from the piano, and taking up a much-read copy of Emerson, pulled the boy onto her lap and read: "The common experience of man is, that he fits himself as well as he can to the customary details of that work or trade he falls into, and tends it, as a dog turns a spit. Then is he a part of the machine he moves — the man is lost." Turning to another page — much read and underlined — she read again: "Each man has his own vocation. The *talent* is the *call*. There is one direction in which all space is open to him. He has faculties silently inviting him thither to endless exertion. He is like a ship in a river; he runs against obstruction on every side but one; on that side all obstruction is taken away and he sweeps serenely over God's depths into infinite sea." "It had been my desire, son," said the mother, "that you make law your profession; but if any talent calls you in another direction,

A Chapter from a Boy's Life.

follow it, dear, as *God's call*." A few days later, the boy was the proud possessor of a beautiful flute. True to his conviction, without instruction, clear and sweet were the tones he produced, as in perfect harmony he followed each selection upon the piano. For a year, now, he has studied under Theodore Hahn, Cincinnati's finest flutist; and as a beautiful statue grows under the hands of a sculptor, so the boy's talent assumes the proportion of genius under the instruction of the artist. This is but a chapter from a boy's life. It is a life so pure, so beautiful, that, like a ray of sunshine, it sheds light upon all about it. And in the language of Emerson: "When we see a soul, whose acts are all regal, graceful and pleasant as roses, we must thank God that such things can be and are."

HOW THE
CAPTAIN FOUND HIS SERVANT

(A Tale from Southern Life)

* * *

I WAS seated in that snug little recess on the second floor of the Atlantic Hotel at Norfolk, Va. (a spot much sought by its guests because of the beautiful marine view it affords), chatting with Captain W—, one of Norfolk's oldest and best-known citizens, who resides in the same mansion occupied by his family for five generations.

The Captain possessed, in a marked degree, that distinguished bearing peculiar to the Southern soldier, and which upon this occasion was accentuated by his uniform of Confederate gray. He apologized for wearing it to call upon me, stating that he had just been attending the funeral of a comrade, and that the entire camp wore their uniforms. I assured him his appearance needed no apology; that to me the garb of Confederacy was more royal than the robe of a king.

The Captain chatted of Norfolk, of its wonderful commercial interest, and of its advantages over other Virginia cities, being a seaport town. I fully coincided with him that no city in the South was more progressive than Norfolk. At this juncture of our conversation a pianette in the street below began loudly playing "All Coons Look Alike to Me."

"I declare," said the Captain. "In the language of Polk Miller, 'all coons may look alike to some, but they don't to me.' I'll say this, however, the shiftless, unreliable negroes of the present age are astonishingly alike, and altogether different from the servants of the old South, who partook to a certain extent of the individuality of their owners, and who are fast becoming a feature of the past."

"Is it true, Captain," I asked, "that after more than a quarter of a century you found your old body servant whom you supposed to have been killed at Sharpsburg?"

Found his Servant.

"True as Gospel, and stranger than any fiction," he replied.

"I never learned the particulars, I should love to hear the story," I suggested.

"It came about in this way," replied the Captain, drawing his chair nearer mine and settling himself into a more comfortable position.

"I was visiting a western town on business, and while there was the guest of General H——, who was a very gallant soldier in the Union army, and, as the wont of soldiers, we fell to discussing war times. 'I tell you,' said the General, 'we have an old darkey here for whom I always feel a deep pity. It seems he was the body servant of some Confederate soldier who was killed at Antietam, and to whom he had been so attached that the master's death completely unbalanced his mind. He was taken prisoner and brought North, and could never tell anything save that he "lived in ole Virginny," and "b'long'd to Marse Capt. and now Marse Capt. dade he doan b'long no place."'

"'Is he a Virginia negro?' I asked. 'From this and certain Virginia provincialisms, I take it he is,' answered the General.

How the Captain

"'If he is a Virginia negro I must look him up,' I replied. The General rang for his porter and dispatched him in quest of the old darkey, whom an hour later he ushered into our presence. A typical old Virginia darkey I found him, save for the 'unbalanced condition' of which the General had spoken.

"When I made known to him that I was from Virginia, his dazed brain seemed momentarily to brighten, and he asked, 'Does you all know my Marse Capt., what killed at Sharpsburg?' Being unable to place him, the old slave relapsed into his semi-conscious state.

"'I tell you,' said the General, 'get him off on some of his tales about Marse Captain, when they were boys, and he seems sane enough. He seems alive only to the past. Life seems to have stopped for him with the death of his master.'

"'What do you remember best about Virginia?' I asked. The old darkey's face brightened.

"'I reckon I members bes' when Marse Capt. an' we all's boys; an' ole Marse done come mammy's cabin one mawnin, an' he put he han'

Found his Servant.

on my haid, an' he say: "You all come 'th me, boy. I done gwine kayh you all to big house. You gwine hab new Marse." An' sho' 'nuff, ole Marse done kayh me big house, an' de fiddles was a scrapin', an' de table done full ob de mos' scrumtifyinest eatens. Um—uh! an' a big cake sot in de middle ob de table, wif ten candles burning on 't. An' ole Marse done call little Marse up, an' he say: "I done bring you all Jim fo' you birfday gift. This Jim's birfday, too. You all bof ten years old to-day, an' I gwine mek you present ob Jim fo' yo' Sarvent to wait on you, an' tek care on you. But mine, you has to be kine to Jim; an' you, Jim, you mus' 'bey yo' new Marse. You done b'long to him now. You doan b'long me no mo'." Gord! but dat boy pow'ful tickled. He say he reckon I finest present he ever got sho' 'nuff. After we all's dinner, he kayh me to woods, toten' he gun, jes' as proud an' big as ole Marse hesef. Lawd! ole Marse was de proudest lookin' man in all Virginny; an' little Marse de zactinest picter ob he. I was pow'ful proud dat day, too, toten' my new Marse's gun; an' mammy an' Mistis, mos' as satisfractious as we all, stan'in' in de gyardin smilin', an' watchin' little Marse walkin' off so proud-like, with me an' de dawgs foll'in' he, jes' fo' all the wuld like ole Marse hesef. Gord! reckon I nevah fergits when some po' white trashes boys got me an' Marse into disgracefulness. Um—uh! mebbe ole Marse didn' wear we all out; an' Mistis 'mos' done stracted an' tuk to de baid fo' week. Little Marse took we all's thrashin' pow'ful to heart, but mammy tuk we all in de pantry an' done pacify our feelins wid cake and mince-pie. Um—uh! Reckon I take thrashin' now to get some mammy's ole Virginny cookins.'

"The old darkey paused, and I felt myself tremble as I seized the General's arm.

"'This is my old family slave, General, I have not the shadow of a doubt,' I exclaimed. 'What! can it be possible?' asked the General.

"'What occasioned the disgrace, boy?' I asked. But the old darkey's mind had wandered again. He shook his head and muttered: 'Marse Capt. dade at Sharpsburg. I is kayh'd way, nebbah see ole Virginny no mo'.' He subsided into silence again. I touched his arm, 'You were both whipped for having your arms tattooed.'

Found his Servant.

A gleam of conscious remembrance flitted across his countenance, and rolling up his ragged sleeve, he bared a dusky arm, revealing his name and date of tattoo. I seized the old darkey in my arms, and sobbed aloud; baring my own arm, I showed a similar date, and my own name.

"'Look at me, Jim,' I cried, leading him under the full light of the chandelier, 'Who am I?'

"'Good Gord A'mighty,' he exclaimed; 'it's ole Marse hesef.'

"I pointed to his own reflection in an opposite mirror, 'Come, boy,' I exclaimed, 'you *must* understand, do you not see how white *your own hair has grown?* We were children together. I am your young master. When the Yankees captured you and took you from my side where I lay prostrate and bleeding on the field of Sharpsburg, I was not dead, as you supposed, but only wounded. Poor fellow, the shock has turned your faithful brain. Come, Jim, we are going to dear old Virginia again.' The old fellow clung to me with the helplessness of a child.

"'Gord A'mighty, Marse!' he sobbed, 'I is pow'ful glad to see you all again, but you alls

How the Captain Found his Servant.

po' mine mus' be done 'stracted, tryin' mek me bleev you all Marse Capt. Gord! Marse, I powful glad to see we alls family once mo'.'

"When we returned to Norfolk, and I carried the old fellow to visit the grave of my father, he insisted it was 'Young Marse's grave,' and until the day of his death, two years subsequent, the faithful old servant spent most of his time beside the grave at the foot of which he now sleeps."

"There is no fiction equal to reality," I exclaimed, as the captain closed his story. "None," he replied, "and as I witness the new ways of a new South, and realize that I stand alone among the few who belong to the old ante bellum days which are gone forever, it helps soothe my grief when the coffin-lid closes upon the face of my comrades, for it means a reuniting with them in another world."

As he arose to go, extending a hand in cordial good-bye, while in the other he held the broad-brimmed hat of Confederate gray, I looked at the splendid courtly gentleman of the old régime, and sighed — that all too fast they are passing away.

THE BRIDAL CHAMBER

OF FLORIDA'S SILVER SPRINGS

NEAR Florida's celebrated Silver Springs lives an old negress, known to the entire surrounding community as "Aunt Silly," and whose claim to being one hundred and ten years old is borne out by her appearance. Aunt Silly is wrinkled and decrepit, and the wool peeping from her bandannaed head is white as snow, while the blackness and weirdness of her face is intensified by a heavy crop of snow-white beard. As long as the oldest citizens of Ocala and surrounding vicinity can remember, Aunt Silly has looked just as ancient as she does now; identified always with Silver Springs, and hobbling about them from morning until night, leaning upon her short thick staff. That she was participant in a tragedy, is known only to a very few of Ocala's oldest citizens,

The Bridal Chamber.

and seldom referred to by any of them. In the near vicinity of Ocala, when first it was settled, stood a splendid old mansion, owned by Captain Harding Douglass, a South Carolinian of considerable wealth. His only child was a son, who with his mother's beauty of countenance, had inherited her tender, shrinking nature, and, like herself, was a slave to the old man's iron will. In the beautiful little city of Ocala lived Bernice Mayo, whose blonde beauty won, at first sight, the heart of Claire Douglass. Although of Virginia ancestry, Bernice was a true child of the "Land of Flowers," passionate and impulsive. Her eyes were blue and clear as the waters of Lake Munroe, beside which she had spent her childhood in the fair little city of Sanford. Her hair was as golden as Florida's own sunshine, and Florida's tropical splendor ran riot in her blood. For six months, Bernice Mayo and Claire Douglass were constant companions, and Silver Springs was their favorite resort. For half a day at a time they would drift about on the bosom of the splendid, placid curiosity of nature.

Bernice seemed never to tire of gazing into

The Bridal Chamber.

the depths of this subterranean world. "If I were a mermaid, Claire," she would say, "and lived in yon crystal cavern, and some fair day I should wander forth among the palmettos and mosses of the Springs, and, sitting on yonder ledge of rock, should 'comb my golden hair with a shell,' and your boat should come drifting by, and you see me in the water beneath, would you love me well enough to plunge — plunge to the depths beneath to woo me?" Then would Claire stop her merry chatter with his kisses, and pledge to her his eternal love, as they drifted over the transparent mirror of water, pausing now and then to study the rocks and shells, the mosses, palmettos, and fish, which were as visible eighty feet beneath the transparent water as were the trees and woodland about them. There is nothing fairer than Ocala's "Lovers' Lane," and yet no spot held for these young people the attraction of Silver Springs — their constant trysting spot. But there came a fatal day — destined to separate them. A day wherein Claire Douglass declared to his father his love for beautiful, penniless Bernice Mayo, and his determination to make

The Bridal Chamber.

her his wife. Stormily his father vowed it should never be, and secretly planned a separation. When Claire Douglass had been speedily dispatched abroad on important business for his father, then it was that Bernice learned the truth, and her proud, delicate nature lay crushed and bleeding beneath the cruel blow and still more cruel separation. Vainly she strove to rally; all life seemed but an empty blank to her.

A year dragged wearily by, and the scenes frequented by merry Bernice Mayo knew her no more. Paler and thinner she daily grew. Fragile she was as the white blossoms of her well-loved Springs. The little chain of gold Claire had locked upon her arm would have slipped across the wasted, transparent hand but for the ribbon which held its links. One day (her last upon earth) the girl by dint of desperate energy crept to the station and boarded the train for Silver Springs. Even old Aunt Silly was unprepared for the white, emaciated little creature who tottered into her cabin door and fell fainting in her arms. Consciousness soon returned; but it was apparent even to

The Bridal Chamber.

the old black woman that death had set his gray, unmistakable seal upon the young face. "Aunt Silly," gasped the girl, "I have come to you to die, and you must obey my last request; the grave divulges no secrets. Ere to-night's sun sets, I shall be in heaven. This separation from the man I love has been my death — but *in that death* — we shall be *reunited*. I have asked God — and he has heard me. But you — Aunt Silly — you must obey my request. You loved me — you will do as I ask you. To-night — when the moon comes out — row my body to Boiling Spring, and bury me there. You know the spot — *make no mistake*. *Do this*, and *God* will attend to the rest." "Good Gord A'mighty, chile, you think Aunt Silly am gwine tote dade body off in de lonesomely night?" asked the old woman, her very teeth chattering with the superstitious fear peculiar to her race. The girl realized the risk of her plan being thwarted, and raising herself to a sitting posture, she seized the old woman's hands and fixed her dying eyes full upon her face.

"Aunt Silly," she gasped, "I am a dying woman — I am very near to God — I have talked

The Bridal Chamber.

with Him — and He has answered me. My will has been crushed in life — I swear it shall not be in death. Before twenty-four hours Claire Douglass shall join me in the crystal cavern of Silver Springs. If you do not grant my request every spirit of evil shall surround you. Palsied and blind you shall grow — and deaf; deaf to every sound but the ghosts of the dead, which shall pursue you by day and haunt you by night. Do you *swear* to obey my dying request — or will you refuse me — and reap the prophecy of a dying woman, which shall rest upon your cowardly head — for refusing to obey God's will." The old woman was shaking like an aspen. Her eyes protruded with fear, and great beads of perspiration rolled down her cheeks. The strength of the dying girl's will had prevailed, and the old woman answered: "I promises, honey, — I promises." It was a solemn and awful sight that night, witnessed alone by God and nature, the boat — which drifted down Silver Springs in the moonlight, bearing its two strange occupants. The one — weird, bent and grotesque; the other — so silent, so white, so pathetic, in its dead loveliness.

The Bridal Chamber.

Not a leaf was stirring — not a sound heard — but the plash — plash of the old woman's oars, as her boat, with its strange, beautiful burden, drifted down the curious, transparent body of water. Drifted until it reached Boiling Spring, then veered about, and stood still. Gently, and easily as if it had been a babe, the old woman lifted the little body. Something of her fear had departed — in the placid smile of the sweet, dead face. Tears rolled down her dusky cheeks, as she bent forward in obedience to the girl's curious request. For a moment the body rocked to and foe on the bosom of the water upon which its happiest moments had been spent. The dead face smiled, and the wealth of hair gleamed in the moonlight like a sheen of gold. Every pebble was visible in the depth below. Suddenly, as if by magic, the body began sinking. The boiling of the spring had ceased, showing the peculiar little fissure in the rock from whence all the strange body of water came. The fissure slowly divided, received the dead body and closed again, shutting every vestige of it from view. "Gord A'mighty! Dat chile a angel sho nuff. She

The Bridal Chamber.

mus done talked de Lawd sho', to knowed how all dat gwine be," muttered the old woman, as she rowed back to her cabin in the moonlight. A mocking bird on the opposite shore sent forth a flood of silver melody. "Hear dat now," muttered Aunt Silly, "dat bird done sendin' foth he weddin' song fo' de bridegroom. Come on Claire Douglass — yo' little bride am waitin' for you more pacifyin den she waited many long day."

The day following the death of Bernice Mayo was one never to be forgotten by the citizens of Ocala. Claire Douglass had just returned after a year's absence. He found his beautiful cousin (whom his father desired to become his wife) a guest at the home of his parents. "Claire," said the father, as they lingered over the breakfast table, "I have a fine new launch at Silver Springs, and I wish you to take your cousin for a sail this morning, and, by the permission of you young people, I shall make one of your party." "Delightful, uncle!" cried the girl, and Claire, while he turned a trifle pale at the thought of returning to the spot where all that had given color to his life had trans-

The Bridal Chamber.

pired, could only acquiesce. Claire Douglass looked unusually handsome as the party drifted down Silver Springs in the April sunshine, but there was a curious pallor upon his face — and the uncle and niece were left to carry on all the conversation. What a contrast the blooming girl in the April sunshine bore to the one in the solemn moonlight who had drifted over the same water the evening before. As the launch neared Boiling Spring, the party noted a little boat hovering over it. The boat was rowed by Aunt Silly; and its other occupant was an old woman whose eyes were swollen with weeping. The launch paused beside the little rowboat, and the occupants of each gazed into the curious, transparent depths below.

Suddenly the niece cried out, "Oh, see! that looks like a hand, a little human hand." Plainer and more visible it grew, the little white hand with its gold chain locked about the slender wrist. Ah, little hand! Claire Douglass would have known you among ten thousand hands. His face was white as death, and he gasped, as though choking. All were intent upon the scene below. Suddenly the boiling of the water ceased,

The Bridal Chamber.

and out upon a rock in its transparent depth, like a broken, beautiful lily, lay Bernice Mayo, her golden hair floating on the sand, her dead face smiling placidly as if — at last a halo of peace had descended upon the tired spirit, and the broken heart had found rest. With a wild cry, which pierced even the heart of the mother, who for the last time in life gazed upon the dead face of her child, Claire Douglass dashed overboard, diving deeper — ever deeper — until he caught in his arms the little figure of his dead love. Then — once more the rock divided, and closed, shutting from view forever, the lovers, who lay locked in each other's embrace. And again the water whirled and boiled in its mad fury, as if to defy the puny will of him who would have separated what God had joined together. As for the first time the secret bridal chamber of Silver Springs has been made known to the world, it will be interesting to its future visitors, as they approach that part of it known as "Boiling Springs," to note in the whirr of water beneath (the only portion of the springs not perfectly placid) the constant shower of tiny pearl-like shells poured forth from the fissure

The Bridal Chamber.

in the rock, and which Aunt Silly says are the jewels the angels gave Bernice Mayo upon her wedding morning, when her lover joined her in their fairy palace in Silver Springs. There is, too, a curious flower growing in the Springs. A flower with leaf like a lily, and blossom shaped like an orange bloom. Its peculiar waxy whiteness and yellow petals are like Bernice Mayo's face and hair, Aunt Silly says, and she calls them "Bernice bridal wreath." There is a legend among the young people of Ocala, that a woman presented with one of these blossoms, shall become a bride ere the close of the year.

POEMS

"Behold! the image cold seemed to have grown
Into real life—a woman, sweet and fair."

TEMPTATION

Chanted was the last Ave Maria,
    Annunciation Feast was at a close,
And round the altar of the Virgin bless'd,
    The fragrance of the incense still arose.

And dense the subtle waves of sweet perfume,
    In soft and filmy clouds still lingered there,
As though they would obscure from all rude gaze
    The Virgin's face, so chaste, so meekly fair.

Deep-toned, the vesper bell rang out its song,
    And woke an echo to the melody
In hearts of all save one, and that the priest's,
    Who knelt alone in silent litany.

Soft, one by one the stars begemmed the sky,
    And through the windows moonbeams weird
        stole in,
And still the silent priest beheld them not,
    Alone with Christ — he fought against his sin.

Temptation.

As stifling as a tomb had grown the church,
    The passion pictures all along the nave
Breathed ghastly fancies to the heated brain
    Of him whom Satan sought to claim his slave.

When lo! Cathedral walls seemed to dissolve,
    And nature, fresh and fair from God's own hand,
Spread o'er his head her canopy of blue,
    And at his feet rich trophies of the land.

Bright hued the butterflies went flitting by,
    And birds made gay the woodland with their song,
While sweet the old-time scent of wild flowers came,
    And sweet came memories that had slumbered long.

Sharp dropped the rosary from his trembling hand,
    For kneeling there before the Virgin's throne,
He felt a human breath soft kiss his cheek,
    Behold! the image cold seemed to have grown

Into real life — a woman, sweet and fair;
    The swelling bust, the snowy neck and arm,
The golden hair, a fitting picture, made
    To suit the scene, and thus complete its charm.

"The fair dream picture vanished from his view,
And with it, sin cast off her blooming mask."

Temptation.

The red lips smiled, the white hand clasped his
    own;
He shivered, and his face grew white as death;
A mighty wind seemed to o'ersweep his frame,
    And from his parchèd lips, hard came his breath.

Soft as the gentle finger-tips of sleep
    On weary eyes, yet keen as scorching fire,
Her hand's electric touch thrilled every vein,
    And left him overpowered with mad desire

To seize and clasp her in his close embrace,
    And in one long, sweet kiss, forget the vow
To priesthood's claim, and pillowed on her breast,
    His lips on hers, live only in the now.

The fair dream-picture vanished from his view,
    And with it, sin cast off her blooming mask,
And stood unsheathed in all her ugliness,
    And mocked, and taunted him as if to ask —

Of what avail were sacred oath and vow,
    If, like a mighty wind o'er sweeping reed,
The flower-soft touch of one fair woman's hand
    Could overweigh the strength of church's
        creed?

. . . .

Temptation.

The first faint flush of dawn blushed in the east,
    And through cathedral windows trembled fair,
Until it shed a halo on the head
    Of him who wrestled all night long in prayer.

And when the Angelus pealed forth its call,
    And brought the people to the church once more,
They gazed upon the priest in fear and awe,
    Amazed at the angelic look he wore.

"They gazed upon the priest in fear and awe,
Amazed at the angelic look he wore."

VILLANELLE

Oh, dainty, sweet-breathed jasmine flower,
   I read the message passing well,
Ye brought from fragrant southern bower;

Brought to my heart with magic power,
   From voice more southern sweet than thou,
Oh, dainty, sweet-breathed jasmine flower.

And not for earth's most tempting dower,
   Would I exchange the message sweet
Ye brought from fragrant southern bower.

I seem to feel a golden shower
   Of southern sunshine warm in thee,
Oh, dainty, sweet-breathed jasmine flower.

I dream — nor heed the passing hour;
   From Cupid's cup I drain the draught,
Oh, dainty, sweet-breathed jasmine flower,
Ye brought from fragrant southern bower.

I MISS YOU SO

(Respectfully dedicated to Mrs. George Howell Finn)

The ocean tosses at my feet,
   I love its ebb and flow,
And yet its burden seems to be,
   I miss you — miss you so.

Upon its bosom sails a ship,
   It stately drifts, and slow,
It bears a missive saying, dear
   I miss you — miss you so.

Upon my breast a crimson rose
   Breathes sweet, as zephyrs blow,
But e'en its incense seems to say,
   I miss you — miss you so.

The moon in sky-land meadow drifts
   O'er sea, in bed of snow,
And yet its brightness saddens me,
   I miss you — miss you so.

MISSISSIPPI ON THE GULF

(PASS CHRISTIAN, MISS.)

My heart is jest a-pinin' fer the South,
    A-longin' an' a-achin' fer to see
The sun a gleamin', streamin' through the leaves
    Of lilac-blossomed china-berry tree.

A-longin' fer the jasmine's incense sweet,
    The honeysuckle, an' the pinewood's green,
The gulf a-lashin', dashin' on the beach,
    Where loungin' you can catch the sea air keen.

An' when upon the gulf the moonlight sleeps,
    The water gleams a-tremblin' bed of white,
An' clear the mock-birds sing an' ring their song,
    Athwart the odorous stillness of the night.

Oh, dear old Mississippi on the gulf,
    My heart is just a-achin' fer to see
The sunlight driftin', siftin' through the leaves
    Of creamy-blossomed, tall magnolia tree.

WHY DANDELIONS TURN GRAY

A FINE young lord came flitting by,
   Gold-coated bumblebee;
He gayly humm'd an old love-song,
   A sad, sad flirt was he.

Upon a dandelion he smiled,
   And praised her yellow hair,
And vowed if she would grant a kiss
   Allegiance he would swear.

The dandelion her fair face hid
   Within her golden hair,
And deemed it strange a gay young lord
   Should find plebeian fair.

"No Loves but vagrant winds have I,"
   She said with tossing head,
"And should I give to you a kiss,
   'Twould not be missed," she said.

Why Dandelions Turn Gray.

Close by a little violet,
    Shamed — drooped her azure eyes;
The lily hung her modest head,
    The rose blushed with surprise.

A listening bird sang overhead,
    "Oh, dandelion, beware,"
While at her feet a katy-did,
    Sharp chirped, "take care — take care."

But recked she not their warning notes,
    Nor heeded flowers' surprise,
Her silly heart was proud, that she
    Found grace in royal eyes.

The lord then kissed her fragrant lips,
    Caressed her golden hair,
And whispered that, midst all the flowers,
    She reigned the queen most fair.

And every day more vain she grew,
    In that her wond'rous charms
Should lift her from a humble lot,
    And give her coat of arms.

But as the summer glided by
    Her heart with fear grew numb,
For promises that were not kept,
    And lord who did not come.

Why Dandelions Turn Gray.

And all her golden locks turned gray,
    Her face grew blanched with fear,
Lest ne'er again her lover's voice
    In rapture she should hear.

In woe she cried unto the gods,
    "If my Love's false, I pray
Ye bid Hermes come unto me,
    And waft my soul away."

She turned about, and there beheld
    His lordship at her side,
His mouth all sweet with choice perfume,
    From lips of moss-rose bride.

And lo! unto her Hermes came,
    And bore her soul away,
Unto Olympus' snowy heights,
    Where reigns eternal day.

And since she trifled thus with Love,
    The debt her race must pay
By forfeiting their golden locks;
    So — dandelions turn gray.

And thus it is with maid or flower
    Whose love's not well bestowed,
The fetter, though a band of gold,
    The victim's soul must goad.

LINES TO A BEAUTIFUL GIRL

SHAKE out your fragrance, dew-drenched rose,
    Breathe soft your incense, jasmine sweet,
Bear them, O breeze, in fragrant kiss,
    To Flossie, fair, on wings so fleet.

The whiteness of the lily fair,
    The warmth of crimson-hearted rose,
The grace and beauty of the gods,
    In lovely Flossie all repose.

The quiet of cathedral dim,
    The joyous music of the birds,
Are Flossie's:—She a symphony
    Set to a poem of sweet words.

AWAY DOWN IN GEORGIA

A MOUNTAIN lad and lassie fair,
As free from care as birds in air,
A lovely, thoughtless, happy pair,
 Away down in Georgia.

Untaught, the lad, in worldly way,—
The lass coquettish, wild and gay;
She broke a heart in sportive play,
 Away down in Georgia.

Long years have come and gone since then;
The mountain lad of "Jasmine Glen"
Is shrewdest of the legal men,
 Away down in Georgia.

A woman lone, in foreign clime,—
A statesman, in his manhood's prime,—
Each sighing for "the auld lang syne,"
 Away down in Georgia.

Away Down in Georgia.

When they were lad and lassie fair,
As free from care as birds in air,
A lovely, thoughtless, happy pair,
    Away down in Georgia.

PROTEST

Ah, ye, whose souls dwell not among the clouds,
    Who cull not bright-hued fancies from the flowers,
Hear not sweet music wafted on the breeze,
    What know ye of this mystic world of ours?

What know ye of the fierce intensity
    Of Pleasure? (god-born nymph for which we weep,
And slay King Reason in a single quaff
    From Cupid's cup, with which our souls we steep.)

Then judge us not, ye folks of mundane sphere;
    Your earth-bound feet can never hope to press
The "milky way" of heaven, that path of gods,
    Nor touch the bright-hued train of Iris' dress.

VILLANELLE

'Neath a sunbonnet smiled my face,
   "Fresh as a rose," my sweetheart said;
'Neath a sunbonnet soft with lace.

"Like flower in an exquisite vase,
   Or jewel rich and rare," he said,
'Neath a sunbonnet smiled my face.

And he said that my "roguish grace"
   Made him my "captive," when I smiled
'Neath a sunbonnet soft with lace.

And now I smile from jeweled case,
   He caught me with his cam'ra, when—
'Neath a sunbonnet smiled my face,
'Neath a sunbonnet soft with lace.

"It shall live in song and story,
Though its folds are in the dust."

THE STARS AND BARS

The bonny flag, the stars and bars,
    The dear old flag we loved so well,
Our flag immortal, for 'twill live
    Always in tales that poets tell.

Aye! more than this; 'twill ever live
    In every throb of Southern heart,
In tender love — more priceless far
    Than bloomless laurels could impart.

The Stars and Bars.

Not only shall its mem'ry live
   In noble hearts that wore the gray,
But cherished, just as tenderly,
   For their dear sakes in after day.

When their brave hearts have ceased to beat,
   And unborn youth their places fill,
The dear old flag, the stars and bars,
   In tenderest love will linger still.

And sons and daughters proudly wear
   Upon their breasts its symbol dear,
While mothers teach their lisping babes
   To reverence the old flag with tear.

ONENESS

You seem so near to-night,
    Your eyes smile into mine
With the same tender light
That made my life so bright
    With sunshine — caught from thine.

And e'en your voice I hear,
    I start — and turn around,
As rich, and full, and clear,
There falls upon my ear
    That magic old-time sound.

I feel your hand clasp mine,
    And tremble at its thrill,
While all the magic grace
Of your proud loving face
    Doth beam upon me still.

Oneness.

And now — glow warm and rich
   Your kisses half divine,
They thrill adown my veins
As might the fiery stains
   Of some rich, rare old wine.

And is this but a dream?
   Ah no, o'er time and space,
O'er stretch of land and sea,
You'll ever come to me
   In all your magic grace.

ECHO

(Dedicated to Lucretia Heine Zink, aged three, who gave inspiration to the poem.)

A BABY face with tear-wet eyes
    Leaned o'er a deep-curbed well,
"I'd det you wif a stick," she cried,
    "If I knew where you fell."

"Is it your doll, my love?" said I;
    She shook her golden head,
"I'll det her wif a great big stick,
    It's Echo, dear," she said.

"Dear little Echo that loves me;
    Now hark! 'I love you!' hear?"
And up from out the deep old well,
    Came "love you," soft and clear.

"Echo's a water nymph, my sweet,
    And that's her home," said I;
If you should bring her here to live,
    Poor little thing would die.

Echo.

"She lives down deep in Crystal Cave,
   In home that's bright and fair."
"She's happy then!" the baby said,
   "I dess I'll leave her there."

And thus it is with sage and seer;
   They smile and weep in vain,
Not knowing that the grief or joy
   But echoes their own brain.

WHAT HER SISTER THOUGHT

I wouldn't dive *my* pretty doll
    To Echo in the well,
Nor dive gold buttons to the goose,
    If out my dwess they fell,

Like 'Cretia did; for when next year
    Dear Santa makes our tree,
He'll find all 'Cretia's things are gone
    And then he'll say — "Oh me!

She didn't keep a single thing
    I bringed to her last year;
I dess this time I'll have to dive
    Them to her Sister dear."

And so I will not dive *my* doll
    To Echo in the well,
Nor feed the gooses buttons gold,
    If out my dwess they fell.

CLEOPATRA

Here, Charmion! unbind my locks,
   And let their bright luxuriant fold,
Sweep unconfined — in glittering mass,
   Bedecked in Egypt's regal gold.

My robe of finest texture bring,
   With filmy lace, and jewels rare,
That Cleopatra may to-night,
   Amongst the fairest, reign most fair.

And then, by all the gods I swear,
   When Rome's proud ruler 'gain we greet,
Despite his honor or his land,
   Meek he shall kneel at Egypt's feet.

Your virtue, cold Octavia,
   Your station proud — and you his wife,
Can never bind great Antony,
   For mine he is — and mine for life.

Cleopatra.

In wildest triumph swells my heart,
    And fire seems coursing through my veins,
Kindling anew old thoughts and dreams,
    Recalled from mem'ries long-lost strains.

Haste then! ye lagging moments, haste!
    And bring proud Antony to my feet,
With all the passion of his love,
    With all his ardent wooing sweet.

Bring back to me my Roman love,
    My princely ruler, warrior bold,
E'en now he loves me better far,
    Than people, country, fame or gold.

Haste then, my gentle Charmion,
    Bring richest robe, and gems most rare,
That Cleopatra may to-night,
    Amongst the fairest, reign most fair.

RETROSPECTION

(Dedicated to Lulu Bainbridge Zink.)

Just ask old Time to stand aside;
   Swing wide his curtain, sister mine,
And fairy-pinioned let us drift
   Again to childhood's glad playtime;

To childhood's simple guileless joys,
   When bird or flower called forth a smile,
When we knew not a single care,
   Nor knew the world's deceit and guile.

Old Time!— thy curtain wider sweep,
   Grudge not to me this slight request,
There— little sister, can you see
   How gay the fields and woods are dressed?

Our playhouse in the garden, too,
   Beneath yon clump of lily bloom,
Where gladsome summers swiftly sped,
   And our young hearts were all attune

Retrospection.

To summer's poesy and song;
    Ah! childish dreamers we, and quaint,
Methinks I ofttimes catch the smell
    Of those same flowers, that memories paint.

Yet, since on ocean, I my bark
    With boldness all her sails unfurl,
This maddened current I'll not shun,
    For calmer harbor — little girl.

REGRET

All evenin' I've been settin' here
    A-cryin' to myself,
Over this ragged little book,
    From off the garret shelf.
It's twenty years an' over now,
    Sence I have seen the book,
I felt so lonely-like to-night,
    I thought I'd go an' look

Fer it; fer somehow all these years
    I've hankered fer that book,
A-layin' there deserted — an'
    Dust covered in its nook.
I couldn't trust my feelin's though,
    An' so I let it lay
All dusty on the garret shelf
    Until this very day.

Regret.

You see it b'longed to little Tom,
    Who died long years ago;
It seems to me but yisterday,
    Though time does drag so slow;
I almost see his little head
    A-bendin' o'er the book,
A-lookin' at the picters there,
    As children like to look.

I almost hear his little voice
    Ring out in merry glee,
As he'd pick out the picters in't
    An' tell uv them to me.
His sunny curls a-tumblin' down
    Jes techin' uv the book,
While he looked at the picters in't
    As children like to look.

The losin' of him, I might stand,
    Though time does drag so slow,
Ef it was not fer what I done
    Mor'n twenty years ago.
One brilin' day in summer time
    When I'd been workin' hard,
A-bakin', an' a-washin', an'
    A-weedin' in the yard.

Regret.

My little Tom came runnin' up,
    A-holdin' of the book,
An' sayin', "See this picter, dear,
    Oh mother! please do look!"
But I was warm, an' awful tired,
    An' didn't want to see,
An' so I turned an' slapped the child,
    An' cried, "Quit botherin' me!"

I still kin see the big tear-drops,
    Come to his little eyes;
But how should I know baby Tom
    Was ripenin' fer the skies?
An' that day wus the very last
    He ever teched the book,
He went an' put it on the shelf
    With sech a sorry look.

An' that night he wus taken sick,
    An' all the time he'd say,
"Oh mother, I won't bother you,
    I'll take my book away."
I hear it durin' all the day,
    I hear it all the night;
It comes to me with every sound,
    It comes with every sight;

Regret.

An' when I'm settin' here alone
    An' mem'ries round me crowd,
An' th' clock ticks so lonesome-like,
    An' sounds all seem so loud,
It's then I see the little face,
    So dimpled, an' so fair,
The big blue eyes brim-full of tears,
    The curly yaller hair,
The little voice draws nearer then,
    So plain it seems to say,
"Oh mother, I won't bother you,
    I'll take my book away."

INFINITE

I have wept in tempestuous fashion
  Till my eyes have grown dim with their
    tears,
Ever striving to crush out a passion
  That must only grow stronger with years.

Heart and brain have held combat together,
  And have waged a war, bitter and strong,
But the brain's reasoning weighs not a feather
  In the heart's current, fiery and strong.

I have wildly implored help from heaven,
  Help to crush down and bury this love,
But I know, should all heaven be riven
  Of its strength and sent down from above,

'Twould avail not; for stronger than this is,
  Is the love that I know cannot die;
And from out of the depth of its blisses,
  Forever and ever 'twill cry.

Infinite.

From my sight oft I think it entombéd,
    So deep down that no eye can discover;
But anon — it will burst forth illuméd,
    All too fair, for such uncanny cover.

And it bridges all time and all space,
    Ah, yes, all — that can keep us apart;
Till it clasps me in eager embrace —
    Close — so close to its warm beating heart.

And to-night, in the cruel starvation
    Of this pitiless, passionate love,
For one kiss I would barter creation,
    And vie with the joy that's above.

A DARK NIGHT

You all can harp about moonlight,
    As much as ever you please,
Its shinins an' its shadders, how
    They play amongst the trees.

But just give me a pitch-dark night,
    With black clouds in the sky;
You want to know the reason, hey?
    Well! I can tell you *why*.

'Twas on jest such an evenin'; Oh!
    (I mind right well the weath'r),
A lot of us was comin' home
    From dancin' school together.

An' somebody was next to me,
    You needn't ask me who!
An' in the dark he held my hand,
    An' kep' on hold'n it, too,

A Dark Night.

Until we reached the doorstep, an'—
    When he's about to go,
I felt his lips soft pressed to mine,
    An' heard him whisper low:

Somethin' 'at made me — Oh, *so* glad,
    I can't fergit the night,
An' I *know* he would not have said 't,
    If it had been moonlight.

So you can harp about moonlight,
    As much as ever you please,
Its shinins an' its shadders, how
    They play amongst the trees.

But jes give me a pitch-dark night,
    With clouds a-rollin' grand,
An' my sweetheart walkin' with me,
    A-holdin' of my hand.

GOLD *VS.* LOVE

Shake out the trailing sheeny silk,
    Unfold the dainty lace,
Place buds upon her golden hair,
    Just o'er her flower-like face.

Make fast these gems upon her arms,
    These in her shell-like ears;
Heed not the mist o'er her soft eyes,
    Which gem their blue with tears.

And trail the gauzy bridal veil,
    Across her tear-wet eyes,
Forget her proud mouth's quivering,
    Forget her stifled sighs.

From out the gleam of starlit past,
    Into the gloom of now,
There comes from rust of bygone years,
    A face — and broken vow.

Gold vs. Love.

But what's a handsome face and love —
    From out the dreamy past?
Why here are title, land and wealth,
    The things that give one cast.

Then bring ye forth the gray-haired groom,
    So wrinkled and so old,
And pray forget the tearful bride
    Has sold herself for gold.

Come forth, ye tearful, shrinking bride,
    Forget the sweet, dead past,
Accept your title, land and gold,
    The things that give one cast.

LINES TO MY MOTHER

WE miss you as the flowers miss
    The gentle fall of rain,
Or as we miss the roses, or
    The song-bird's sweet refrain.

When evening's purple twilight comes,
    At golden noontide hour,
There's ever something lacking in
    Their splendor and their power.

Even your pet canary, and
    Your parrot, gorgeous green,
Your absence note with silence and
    Would welcome you, I ween,

With burst of song and chatter that
    Will prove that even they
Are glad your long and weary stay
    At length has passed away.

Lines to My Mother.

And as first buds of springtime smile
    Upon our welcome sight,
Or as with pleasure, after dark,
    We hail dawn's rosy light,

We welcome thy dear coming, Oh,
    Thou queen of heart and home;
Our love is like the ocean deep,
    Our pleasure as its foam.

CONTENT

The wind blows keen, the sleet sifts fine,
    Yet merrily I plod along;
My happy heart is keeping time
    To love's sweet pictures set to song.
        Into the night
        There gleams a light
    From yonder cot hard by,
        Where faces dear,
        And hearty cheer,
Both pain and care defy.

I'd not exchange with any king
    His palace for my humble lot,
Where she who wears my wedding-ring,
    Like queen, adorns my humble cot.
        Through sleet and rain,
        From window-pane,
    A form of baby grace,
        With eyes of blue,
        Is peering through
    To spy her daddy's face.

Content.

Oh, baby dear, your sunny hair
    I'd not exchange for misers' gold;
Oh, little wife, no thought of care
    Is mine, when I such treasures hold.
        Athwart the night
        Yon candle bright
    To me is beacon star;
        I haste me fast,
        Through sleet and blast,
    To where my treasures are.

CHASTENED

Whene'er in life the soul's great scale
    Is swept by master hand,
It vibrates to a chord of pain
    We can not understand.

The soul that hears the rhapsodies
    Of heaven while here below,
Must stand alone and view the throng
    Which 'bout him ebb and flow.

Each pain holds bliss, tho' deeply hid,
    Each gift withheld proves joy,
And only life that's hid in Christ
    Finds peace — without alloy.

REVERY

(PABLO BEACH, FLORIDA.)

The green sea dimples in the glowing sun,
    And at my feet soft casts its snowy foam,
As dreamily I gaze far oceanward,
    Nor check my fancies which so idly roam.

Aye! fancies which must ever riot run,
    And paint fair pictures to my famished eyes,
Pictures which rival aught that art can paint,
    And smile again — beneath these Southern skies.

To thee, dear heart, who art so far away,
    Ten thousand tender fancies chant sweet song,
And all in nature that is beautiful,
    My heart and soul cry out, to thee belong.

The softest breeze of this dear "Land of Flowers,"
    Not softer is — than thy sweet Southern voice;
The splendor of thy perfect, matchless soul,
    Nature reflects, and smiles, and does rejoice.

Revery.

Sing on, green sea, and dimple in the sun;
   Trill loud, ye mock-birds, in this land of flowers;
Blow soft, ye fragrant-laden breezes, blow,
   While I dream on — throughout these golden hours.

"I AM THE WAY"

(ST. JOHN 14th — 6.)

Be still, oh earth! and lowly, hark!
    Why will ye walk in grief and pain,
And dull your ears to melody
    Of angel voices' sweet refrain?

For forty years in wilderness
    Toiled Israel — while fair and bright,
Within her very grasp, there lay
    The promised land — a heavenly sight.

So now, before each living soul,
    There stretches pure a peaceful life,
Where troubled waters never roll,
    Nor any earthly care or strife.

When trouble casts its darkened pall
    Athwart thy path excluding day,
Oh burdened soul — but turn to Him
    Who cries to thee, "I am the Way."

"*I am the Way.*"

Oh blessed Way from every care,
   Thou makest night shine forth as day,
When we but realize, Oh Christ!
   That Thou forever art "the Way."

FLORIDA, QUEEN OF THE SOUTH

Oh Florida, thou beauteous queen,
 Of all the South most witching fair;
Upon thy bosom blue lakes gleam,
 Thy brow is crowned with blossoms rare.

Thou art the land of luscious fruit,
 Of tropic trees, and birds, and flowers;
God left the trace of his own hand
 On Florida's enchanted bowers.

Not all the tribute poets bring,
 Oh land of flowers, to thy fair shrine,
Can estimate thy loveliness,
 Or paint one-half those charms of thine.

God must have made thee, oh thou queen,
 His Eden for the sinless pair,
For not a spot on all the globe,
 Did he create one-half so fair.

LINES RESPECTFULLY DEDICATED
TO GENERAL J. J. DICKISON.

A book and bunch of violets,
    Placed in my fevered hand,
As languishing on bed of pain
    I lay in distant land —

In eloquence shall always speak,
    Of tender heart and brave,
Who led his men so valiantly,
    Dear Dixie land to save.

But all the laurels he has won,
    (To those who know him best)
Tell not one-half the story of
    His nature's nobleness.

For this heart that was bravest in
    The battle's fiercest strife,
Sweet radiates the teachings of
    The Master's blessed life.

Dedicatory Lines.

Soon — from o'er all the Land of Flowers,
    The boys who wore the gray,
Shall gather at fair Jacksonville,
    For the "unveiling" day.

To see their hero's statue, which
    Shall ever proudly stand,
To grace the fairest city in
    Fair Florida's bright land.

The frosts of age are on his brow
    But Spring blooms in his heart,
Her blossoms and her sunshine, from
    His soul shall ne'er depart.

Forever shall his valor live,
    In every Southern breast;
His acts of unseen kindness, with
    The ones who know him best.

OCALA, FLA., Feb. 22d, 1898.

THE RED, RED ROSE

Place not within my cold dead hands
    A flower of snowy white,
But give to me the red, red rose,
    All warm with crimson light.

Deck not my bier with any flower
    But with the red, red rose,
And may it breathe to those I love
    My sweetness of repose.

Drape not my door in sable, friends,
    Nor wear the garb of woe;
Why should we mourn, when God Himself
    Has bade a spirit go?

Then place not in my lifeless hand
    A flower of snowy white,
But bring to me the red, red rose,
    All warm with crimson light.

HOW DO I LOVE YOU?

You ask me how I love you, sweetheart mine!
I love you as the birds love fruits' ripe wine.
I love you as the bee loves orange bloom,
Rich laden with the Southland's sweet perfume.

I love you as the parched flowers love the rain,
Which kiss them back to beauteous life again.
I love you as the morning loves the light,
Which dissipates the shadows of the night.

I love you — as a mother babe on breast,
When soft she wooes the fragile thing to rest.
Yet — love you fierce as tiger loves his mate
In jungle, where he roams untamed in state.

I love you as God's Word bids woman love,
With just the worship man gives God above.
And all my will is lost, Oh sweetheart mine,
Forever, in the lightest wish of thine.

TRUST

Between us yawned a gulf we could not bridge,
    We trembled on its brink — and gazed to shore,
For lo! a bright-winged angel hovered there,
    And in his mystic touch our spirits bore,

Beyond the surging tide to sylvan nook,
    Where birds Ave Maria always chant,
And lilies swing their censered incense sweet
    Athwart dream-faces — seen through cloudland slant.

And as God's priests (through Him) speak peace to soul,
    So to us, those pure surpliced, soulless flowers
Spake peace; while chanted all the feathered choir
    God's praise, through nature's green cathedral bowers.

Trust.

And so we clung, and lingered near the gulf
    The brackish waters sweeping at our feet,
While far beyond the angel bore our souls
    To spots where only kindred spirits meet.

In life—'tis ever thus to those who trust—
    They are upheld by mystic spirit hands;
And Christ, in all his blessed tenderness,
    Close to each waiting soul forever stands.

www.ingramcontent.com/pod-product-compliance
Lightning Source LLC
Chambersburg PA
CBHW021352230426
43666CB00006B/494